Bearing Christ's Reproach

Bearing Christ's Reproach

The Challenge of Hebrews in an Honor Culture

by

David A. deSilva

BIBAL Press
North Richland Hills, Texas

BIBAL Press
An imprint of D. & F. Scott Publishing, Inc.
P.O. Box 821653
N. Richland Hills, TX 76182

Copyright © 1999 by David A. deSilva

Printed in the United States of America

03 02 01 00 99   5 4 3 2 1

Library of Congress Cataloging-in-Publication Data

DeSilva, David Arthur.
  Bearing Christ's reproach : the challenge of Hebrews in an honor culture / by David A. deSilva.
      p. cm.
Includes bibliographical references and indexes.
  ISBN 0-941037-86-X (alk. paper)
  1. Bible. N.T. Hebrews—Socio-rhetorical criticism. 2. Honor in the Bible. I. Title.
  BS2775.6.H634 D47 1999
  227'.87067—dc21
                                                    99-006946

Cover image provided by www.arttoday.com

for my wife,
Donna Jean deSilva
with love and gratitude

Contents

Preface

Early Christians faced a number of challenges to persevering in their commitment to the new movement which was spreading throughout the Mediterranean. Rarely during the first century did they experience persecution in the form of official sanctions or executions, but very commonly they faced a variety of levels of unofficial pressure to return to the values and commitments of the culture from which they converted, whether Greco-Roman or Jewish. The Epistle to the Hebrews provides a window into how the larger society applied pressure to early Christians to "shame" them back into conformity with their neighbors, as well as into one Christian leader's strategies for insulating his readers from those pressures. As such, Hebrews becomes an illuminating text for considering how, in every age, to sustain commitment to the Christian world-view and ethos in a non-supportive environment.

This volume is a digest of my doctoral dissertation, *Despising Shame: Honor Discourse and Community Maintenance in the Epistle to the Hebrews* (SBLDS 152; Atlanta, GA: Scholars Press, 1995). I am grateful to Luke T. Johnson, my doctoral advisor, for his guidance and encouragement during the research and writing of that work. I remain indebted as well to Vernon K. Robbins, Carl R. Holladay, and Arthur W. Wainwright, who served on my dissertation committee, for their contributions to my research and thinking. The support of the Society of Biblical Literature, which sponsored the publication of my research first in two articles ("Despising Shame: A Cultural-Anthropological Investigation of the Epistle to the Hebrews," *JBL* 113 [1994] 439–61; "Exchanging Favor for Wrath: Apostasy in Hebrews and Patron-Client Relations," *JBL* 115 [1996] 91–116) and then in its dissertation series, is also acknowledged with appreciation. I am grateful to the SBL for allowing me to make the fruits of that research available here for the non-specialist.

Quotations from classical authors are taken from the Loeb Classical Library unless otherwise noted.

Reading Hebrews within an Honor Culture

The Letter to the Hebrews has been a perennial enigma for scholars. The letter itself gives no certain clues as to the identity of the author, the location of the recipients, the date of composition, or the history and present circumstances of the recipients. As one scholar has observed, the letter itself is like Melchizedek, "without father, without mother, without genealogy."[1] The meaning of leading motifs in Hebrews such as "rest," "perfection," pilgrimage, and faith has been sought by means of thorough examinations of the text against the backgrounds of Gnosticism,[2] Alexandrian Judaism (with particular recourse to Philo),[3] and Jewish-Christian apocalypticism.[4] While many scholars insist on one background over another as the key to interpretation, some rightly argue that such an outlook overlooks "the fluidity of first-century thought."[5] This study proposes another background for the interpretation of Hebrews, one not in competition with the foregoing streams of thought but more basic. This is the cultural background of the importance of honor and dishonor in the Mediterranean world. Such an approach will highlight a dimension of the text which is particularly relevant to the hearers and thus calculated to gain their attention and motivate them to respond to their situation in a particular way.

Over the past two decades, students of both Testaments have begun to mine the insights of cultural anthropology for their work in interpreting the scriptural texts. Cultural anthropology seeks to understand how the people within a given culture give symbolic structure to their perceptions of reality, how they arrange their social interactions into recognizable and predictable patterns, and how they construct systems of values and maintain those values through mechanisms of social control. Anthropologists of the Mediterranean world have found that the concepts of honor and shame are central to the value systems of the cultures occupying that region, and that the people evaluate, make decisions, and approach social interactions in terms of honor and dishonor.

Both classicists and cultural anthropologists have contributed to the development of a picture of the Mediterranean world as an honor-shame culture. A. W. H. Adkins, for example, demonstrates the pervasiveness of concern and competition for honor in the Homeric world (the so-called Heroic Age of the eighth through sixth centuries BCE).[6] The plays of the classical tragedians of fourth-century Athens (i.e., Aeschylus, Euripides, and Sophocles) further demonstrate the survival of honor as a central value. While other values exist for the classical Greeks, consideration of the honorable outweighs considerations of the just or the expedient.[7]

Biblical scholars look particularly to Julian Pitt-Rivers for the beginnings of modern cultural-anthropological reflection on honor and shame in the contemporary Mediterranean. Pitt-Rivers's essay, "Honour and Social Status,"[8] provides the basic components of this model:

> Honour is the value of a person in his own eyes, but also in the eyes of his society. It is his estimation of his own worth, his claim to pride, but it is also acknowledgement of that *claim*, his excellence recognized by society . . . [I]n a complex society where consensus is not uniform, the individual's worth is not the same in the view of one group as in that of another . . . If honour establishes status, the

converse is also true, and where status is conferred by birth, honour derives not only from individual reputation but from antecedence . . . The claim to excel is always relative. It is always implicitly the claim to excel over others. Hence honour is the basis of precedence . . . We should [note] the intimate relation between honour and the physical person. The rituals by which honour is formally bestowed [e.g.] involve a ceremony which commonly centres upon the head of the protagonist . . .

Public opinion forms . . . a tribunal before which the claimants to honour are brought, 'the court of reputation' as it has been called, and against its judgements there is no redress . . . Social groups possess a collective honour in which their members participate . . . [The] head is responsible for the honour of all its members.[9]

From these statements, a picture emerges of the Mediterranean person as a group-oriented person. A person knows and values himself or herself only in connection with a social group and the status or reputation it ascribes to him or her. A person will direct his or her own conduct in accordance with that line of action which will bring approval and recognition of his or her worth in the eyes of the group forming the body of that person's significant others.

Of particular importance is Pitt-Rivers's statement that "in a complex society where consensus is not uniform, the individual's worth is not the same in the view of one group as in that of another."[10] The first-century Mediterranean was just such a complex society, in which the dominant culture, Hellenism, often defined honor differently from many of its subcultures (e.g., Stoicism or Judaism). The maintenance of a minority culture within a dominant culture is a special problem, with discussions of what constitutes *true* honor and who constitutes the *true* court of reputation claiming a prominent place.

Hebrews and Honor

One must be cautious, of course, in applying a model of modern social interactions in the Mediterranean to a text from the Greco-Roman period, two millennia in the past. A reading of Hebrews, however, will quickly demonstrate that the letter itself calls for such an analysis of this dimension of language. First, it contains an abundance of vocabulary and concepts related to honor and dishonor. Words for "reputation" or "opinion" (δόξα), "honor" (τιμή), "dishonor" (αἰσχύνη), "reproach" (ὀνειδισμός), "worthy" (ἀξιός), "outrage" (ὑβρίζω), and related forms appear throughout the first six and last four chapters, forming important connections between sections. Second, the author employs frequently, even centrally, the use of comparison and argument from greater to lesser—two elements of ancient argumentation frequently employed to establish the superior worth of a particular person, the greater honor which would attend a certain course of action, or the greater disgrace which would attend the course of action from which the speaker seeks to dissuade the hearers. The comparative adjective κρείττων, "better," occurs thirteen times in this epistle—more than in all the other New Testament documents combined. The author clearly seeks to establish the superior status and power, and hence honor, of the new dispensation and its agent, Jesus.

Third, and perhaps most striking, is the author's description of Jesus, the supreme exemplar of "faith" (a central value for the author and the Christian community), as one who "endured the cross, despising shame, and sat down at the right hand of God" (12:2 ὑπέμεινεν σταυρὸν αἰσχύνης καταφρονήσας ἐν δεξιᾷ τε τοῦ θρόνου τοῦ θεοῦ κεκάθικεν). Jesus' highly honored position appears to be the result of a certain attitude toward the society's estimation of him—an attitude which the addressees' are called to imitate by "bearing his

Following Christ

reproach" (13:13). How can our author posit the path of dishonor as the road to glory? How can embracing disgrace and reproach from one's society lead to vindication of worth and dignity? Fourth, the author appears to be quite concerned that some of the addressees are in danger of outraging the honor of God. Here we enter into the world of patron-client relationships and the mutual obligations which such a relationship entails (which we will explore more deeply in chapter four). Honoring God, the Patron, is the necessary return for having received God's benefits and the necessary prerequisite for continuing to hope for future benefits. The establishment of this patron-client relationship with God, and the need to continue in the course of action which shows gratitude to the patron rather than contempt for God and his gifts, unifies every section of the letter.

From the abundance of language and concepts expressing a concern for honor and dishonor in Hebrews, we see that, far from being an imposition of a cultural-anthropological model on the text, honor/shame analysis is required for a fuller understanding of Hebrews' challenge to its original hearers. Attention to this realm of discourse will enable us to see with greater clarity how Hebrews sought to persuade its audience, and how Hebrews sought to maintain and fortify its hearers' commitment to the group and its values. Such a line of inquiry will enlighten the situation in which the author and addressees find themselves, and highlight the "manner in which the text is designed through the literary, sociological, and theological strategy of its author(s) to be a specific response to the specific situation of the intended audience as perceived by the author(s)."[11]

Honor and Classical Rhetoric

How can the modern reader "get at" how honor and shame language is at work in Hebrews, and what responses this language would have evoked from its audience? Cultural-anthropological models can help orient one to some basic components of honor in the Mediterranean world, and classical studies can confirm the presence of these components in the ancient Mediterranean, but the interpreter of a text requires something more than heuristic models. The methodological footing we are looking for can be found in large measure in the classical rhetorical handbooks, such as Aristotle's *Art of Rhetoric* and the anonymous *Rhetorica ad Herennium*, and in the analysis of surviving speeches from the Greco-Roman world. These sources have proven to be of great value to the modern interpreter, since they provide insight into how arguments were constructed and what was expected to persuade an audience to adopt or avoid a certain course of action.[12] These handbooks, as well as the speeches left to posterity by a wide variety of orators, can provide specific pointers as to how language about honor and shame could be profitably used on the road to persuasion. Their proximity to the culture of the New Testament authors makes them reliable guides for analysis.

Comparing the components and structure of Hebrews with the advice on constructing persuasive speeches in these handbooks, one cannot fail to observe that this letter is a highly rhetorical document. That is, the author appears to have been aware of "what worked" in oratory and to have composed his letter according to the rhetorical conventions and practices of its period. The letter is written as if intended for oral delivery, using verbs of speaking and hearing rather than writing and reading (unlike, for example, Paul). Hebrews makes notable use of many standard rhetorical compositional devices, such as alliteration (same sound beginning a number of words in close proximity)[13] and anaphora (using a single word repeatedly throughout a section as an emphatic refrain).[14] Hebrews employs many forms of argumentation recognizable from both Greco-Roman and Jewish rhetorical practices: arguments from lesser to greater, comparison, encomium, elaboration on a theme. The work is carefully structured through the use of inclusions (marking off a discrete section of argument by using the same word in the beginning and ending of the section), key terms, and logical connective particles ("therefore," "since"). Since it displays such a high degree of awareness of rhetorical conventions and strategies, we may confidently use the classical rhetorical handbooks and speeches as a guide to its composition and argumentation.

Rhetoricians recognized three genres of speeches: forensic, or courtroom speeches, in which the goal was to convict or acquit; deliberative speeches, in which the goal was to persuade an audience to adopt or refrain from a certain course of action; and epideictic, or demonstrative speeches, in which the goal was the demonstration of a proposition or the praise or blame of an individual. This third category was most directly connected with honor and dishonor. Funeral orations, for example, were occasions to honor the dead for their manner of life, namely the values they displayed in their behaviors and commitments while alive. Such praise of the dead sent a clear message to the hearers: those who live according to these values attain a praiseworthy remembrance after their death, a reputation which, generally, they would have begun to enjoy during their lifetime as well. Funeral orations, or more general praises of a person or group of persons, thus became occasions to remind hearers of the values which were of central importance to the culture, and to motivate the hearers to pursue those values in their own lives because of the honor it will bring them in this life and after death. Indeed, one often finds that funeral orations (or encomia, generally) close with a direct exhortation to the hearers to "imitate" the subjects of the orator's praise.

In the famous funeral oration given by Pericles for the fallen Athenian soldiers in Thucydides' *History of the Peloponnesian Wars* (2.35–44), Pericles praises the dead for their courage in battle, which showed their commitment to the Athenian way of life. This commitment not only preserved the city, but also won for the fallen a noble death and honorable remembrance. The act of honoring the fallen, however, is intended to rouse a similar commitment in the audience, who must continue the fight to preserve the city. Pericles develops at length the greatness of the prize for which the fallen have contended, namely the city-state of Athens with its matchless institutions and way of life. Having set before the eyes of the audience the noble prize for which they, too, are called to contend, he concludes with a direct exhortation:

> You must daily fix your gaze (θεωμένους) upon the power of Athens and must become lovers of her, and when the vision of her greatness has inspired you, reflect that all this has been acquired by men of courage who knew their duty and in the hour of conflict were moved by a high sense of honour . . . For they gave their lives for the common weal, and in so doing won for themselves the praise which grows not old and the most distinguished of sepulchres—not that in which they lie buried, but that in which their glory survives in everlasting remembrance, celebrated on every occasion which gives rise to word of eulogy or deed of emulation . . . Do you, therefore, now make these men your examples . . . For the love of honour alone is untouched by age (2.43.1–4).

Epideictic rhetoric thus appeals to the hearers' own desire for honor, moving them to desire the same opportunity for praise as that enjoyed by the subject of the speech. It encourages them to reaffirm their belief that adherence to the cultural virtues promoted in the speech and embodied by the subject of the speech leads to fulfillment of their desire for honor. Perhaps they will not attain it in battle, but within the constellation of Greek virtues they will have some opportunity. By this epideictic display, they are aroused to avail themselves of that opportunity.[15] Within Hebrews, this feature figures prominently in chapter 11, in which the author directs the addressees' gaze toward the consideration of exemplars of faith, especially Jesus (12:1–3).

This use of language of honor and shame to promote certain cultural values and to proscribe actions which threaten the stability of that culture may be seen also in ethical literature of the Classical and Greco-Roman periods. "Honor" becomes the umbrella which extends over the complex of behaviors, commitments, and attitudes which preserve a given culture and society; the desire for honor becomes the means by which one can motivate the members of that society to seek the good of the larger group as the path to self-fulfillment. In a collection of advice *To Demonicus*, ascribed pseudonymously to Isocrates (a Greek orator from the fourth and third centuries BCE), one finds many actions connected either with the positive sanction "noble" or "honorable," or labeled with the negative sanction "disgraceful." By such means, the author sets before his reader a model of existence which acts always in the best interest of the public trust, which honors the established authorities on which the state rests (gods, parents, laws), and restrains the expenditure of resources on that which brings pleasure only to the self and not benefit to others as well. Those who follow such a model will be rewarded with society's approval and affirmation, that is, honor.

In a very similar manner, the collection of wisdom sayings known as Proverbs inculcates the values essential to the orderly running of society by means of the same sanctions of the honorable and disgraceful. Obedience to parents, the sanctity of marriage, impartiality in the law courts, and integrity in the market are all promoted as the ways to secure a good reputation and honor, while the transgression of the same carries the promise of disgrace. Proverbs, like *To Demonicus*, also seeks to cultivate an interest in respecting the honor and worth of other people—showing deference to social superiors, but also respecting the socially marginal and the poor. The "fear of the Lord," that is, respect for God and an unwillingness to provoke God through arrogance, enforce these attitudes which make for social cohesion rather than division.

Epideictic rhetoric and the closely related ethical literature demonstrate a primary function of honor and shame language in ancient texts—by the use of these categories, authors set out what behavior was valued by and necessary for the group, and motivated people to guide their lives in accordance with these values in such a way that self-interests and group-interests coincide. It should be no surprise, then, to find that honor and shame language play an equally prominent role in deliberative oratory, the genre of rhetoric devoted to persuasion and dissuasion with regard to a particular course of action. This was a similarity noted by the theorists themselves: "praise and counsels have a common aspect; for what you might suggest in counseling becomes encomium by a change in the phrase . . . Accordingly, if you desire to praise, look what you would suggest; if you desire to suggest, look what you would praise" (Aristotle, *Rh.* 1.9.35–36).

Deliberative orators thus sought to prove that the course of action which they recommended would result in greater honor than the course of their opponents, or that the opponents' recommended course of action would result in disgrace.[16] The former would be most readily accomplished by presenting the proposed course as an embodiment of a central cultural virtue, for example one of the four cardinal virtues of the Greco-Roman world: justice, courage, temperance, and wisdom. Alternatively, or additionally, one might provide evidence that such behavior has in the past led to an honorable remembrance for those who have acted out one of these virtues, and so might be expected to do the same for the present audience.[17] Here one finds a valuable place for short passages of epideictic oratory within a deliberative speech, whereby past figures, or a specific virtue itself, are praised as part of a larger attempt to persuade the hearers to adopt a similar course of action.[18]

Deliberative orators sought not only to appeal to the mind (the appeal to *logos*), but also to the emotions of the hearers (the appeal to *pathos*). The rhetorical theorists recognized that people evaluated options and made decisions differently under the sway of different emotions.[19] This is an aspect of the ancient texts that we, in our interest in theology or ethics, might easily overlook, but for the classical orator rousing strategic emotions was the pathway to persuasion. Identifying the emotions being aroused, therefore, can assist the modern reader in the task of discovering what was at stake, what convictions or expectations were being parlayed into emotional expression, and recovering our own ability to engage the text on that level.

Several emotions were closely connected with the values of honor and shame, particularly as these emotions are defined by Aristotle in his *Art of Rhetoric*. The first emotion showing a close connection with considerations of honor is anger. Anger is the expected response to a slight or a show of dishonor when one has a right to expect honor: "Let us then define anger (ὀργή) as a longing, accompanied by pain, for a real or apparent revenge (τιμωρία) for a real or apparent slight (ὀλιγωρία; *Rh.* 2.2.1)." Anger may therefore be roused when an orator suggests that others have acted towards the addressees out of an inappropriately low opinion of their worth. Anger embodies the desire for satisfaction, the reassertion of worth by inflicting some injury or penalty on the offending party. Under what circumstances, and toward whom, are people prone to feel anger when slighted? Aristotle presents as one possibility the improper response of a client: "Men are angry at slights from those by whom they think they have a right to expect to be well treated; such are those on whom they have conferred or are conferring benefits (εὖ πεποίηκεν ἢ ποιεῖ) . . . and all those whom they desire, or did desire, to benefit" (*Rh.* 2.2.8). Within

the patron-client relationship there is the implicit and
inviolable expectation that the benefited will honor the
patron and acknowledge the patron's claim to loyalty and
obedience. If the patron's gifts fail to meet with enduring
honor and esteem, the result will be anger and the accompanying desire for satisfaction, to restore the slighted
honor of the patron.

A second emotion, closely connected with anger, is
fear. If being slighted should arouse anger, making hearers believe they have slighted, or are on the verge of slighting, one more powerful than they should lead to fear:

> Let fear (φόβος) be defined as a painful or troubled
> feeling caused by the impression of an imminent evil
> (κακοῦ) that causes destruction or pain . . . Such signs are
> the enmity and anger (ὀργή) of those able to injure us in
> any way . . . and outraged virtue (ἀρετὴ ὑβριζομένη)
> when it has power, for it is evident that it always desires sat-
> isfaction (*Rh.* 2.5.1, 3, 5).

The greater the person or group slighted, the greater the
fear aroused in the hearers. Where an orator wishes to give
his audience the impression that they are in danger of violating the honor of some person or group, that orator may
heighten the audience's fear by demonstrating the surpassing worth and virtue of the person or group they are in
danger of insulting, and hence the surpassing vengeance
that person or group will exact upon the audience. The
opposite of fear is confidence, which one enjoys when one
has maintained proper relationships with the gods, with
patrons and authorities, and with friends and allies.

Aristotle also lists shame (αἰσχύνη) as an emotion an
orator may find it useful to arouse. An orator may motivate the audience to adopt the course of action he recommends, or to desist from the course of action he
recommends against, by making the addressees feel that
their preservation of a good reputation or reparation of
an ailing reputation depends on it. Similarly, the orator

may motivate the hearers to pursue some recognized good that they might have been expected to have attained already, but have for some reason or other failed to secure, for "it is shameful not to have a share in the honourable things which all men, or all who resemble us, or the majority of them, have a share in" (2.6.12). The author may set up expectations of which the hearers have fallen short in order to motivate them to conduct themselves in the future so as to acquit themselves honorably.

The other side of "shame" is "emulation" (ζῆλος), the desire to preserve one's status and augment one's prestige which one feels when one witnesses the success of another:

> Let us assume that emulation (ζῆλος) is a feeling of pain at the evident presence of highly valued goods, which are possible for us to attain, in the possession of those who naturally resemble us—pain not due to the fact that another possesses them, but to the fact that we ourselves do not. Emulation therefore is virtuous and characteristic of virtuous men, whereas envy is base and characteristic of base men; for the one, owing to emulation, fits himself to obtain such goods, while the object of the other, owing to envy, is to prevent his neighbour possessing them (2.11.1).

Recalling our discussion of epideictic rhetoric, one can see that an orator might incorporate praiseworthy examples in short encomiastic passages, or hold up some good which others have attained as highly desirable, in order to stir up the hearers to emulate those figures and attain those prized goods for themselves.

When one analyzes deliberative speeches from the first century, whether the political addresses of Dio Chrysostom or the speeches in Josephus's *Jewish War*, one finds that the theorists reflect very accurately the actual practice of orators. It should not, therefore, surprise us to discover that the author of Hebrews also uses the language of honor and dishonor in the ways described above. When we turn to the text, we will be attentive to the author's appeals to the hearers' emotions and how these are playing on their desire for honor and the mandate to show proper honor to one's patrons; we will look carefully at the praise and censure of various people and groups as attempts by the author to rouse emulation; we will explore the behaviors and commitments which the author holds up as leading to honor, or from which the author dissuades the hearers as leading to disgrace. We will also be able to discern the values of central importance to this author through the way he connects them with the attainment of honor and its various components.

Honor and the Rhetoric of Minority Cultures

To the insights gleaned from rhetorical criticism outlined above we must also add a social component if we are to understand the use of honor and shame language in Hebrews. Honor and shame are closely linked with the maintenance of the values of the culture. A group exercises a form of social control over its members by rewarding with honor those whose behavior embodies the values central to the preservation of society and by punishing with disgrace those whose behavior violates those values, or at least fails to live up to them. These sanctions function powerfully as motivators.

In a simple society (wherein one culture is shared by all the group members), this process results in a fairly consistent method of social control and predictable adherence to the society's values. The situation becomes more interesting in a complex society, in which one finds competing cultures, or, at least, alternative cultures within a dominant culture. Such, of course, was the Mediterranean world of the first century CE. Within the dominant culture of Hellenism one finds many minority cultures seeking to preserve their distinct identities against one another and against the values and definitions of the dominant (and empowered) culture. In Alexandria, for example, the native Egyptian culture existed alongside the culture of its Hellenistic conquerors together with the transplanted ethnic subculture of Judaism. Throughout the Mediterranean, one sees voluntary subcultures and countercultures, such as philosophical schools and religious sects, striving to maintain their values and group boundaries against competing minority cultures, as well as fighting assimilation back into the dominant culture.

Honor and shame still function in the same way as in a simple society, but with several new operations. First, where the values and commitments of a minority culture differ from those of a dominant (or other alternative) culture, members of that minority culture must be moved to disregard the opinion of non-members about their behavior. All groups will seek to use honor and disgrace to enforce the values of their particular culture, so each must insulate its members from the "pull" of the opinion of non-members. Those who do not hold to the values and the construals of reality embodied in the group are excluded from the "court of reputation" as shameless or errant—approval or disapproval in their eyes must count for nothing, as it rests on error, and the representative of the minority culture can look forward to his or her vindication when the extent of that error is revealed.

We find this frequently in the writings of members of philosophical subcultures in the Greco-Roman world. Plato, for example, frequently contrasts the opinion of the many, who are not guided by a commitment to philosophical inquiry, and the opinion of those few who do examine reality in the light of philosophical truth. In the *Crito*, the title character urges Socrates to have a care for the majority opinion, since it has the power of life and death (displayed so dramatically in Socrates' condemnation). Socrates, however, reminds his friend to care not "so much for what most people think," but rather only "for the most reasonable men, whose opinion is more worth considering" (*Crit*. 44C). "If a man is an athlete and makes that his business, does he pay attention to every man's praise and blame and opinion or to those of one man only who is a physician or a trainer?" he asks. In the same way, the devotee of philosophy cannot allow himself or herself to be guided by the praise and blame of the uninitiated (*Crit*. 46C-47A).

In a similar fashion, Seneca, the first-century Stoic and politician, teaches his pupil that the person seeking to "live according to nature," and to gain "imperturbability" (the chief ends of Stoic philosophy), will not give any weight to the honor or disgrace which the uninitiated show the student of philosophy:

> In the same spirit in which he sets no value on the honours they have, he sets no value on the lack of honour they show. Just as he will not be flattered if a beggar shows him respect, nor count it an insult if a man from the dregs of the people, on being greeted, fails to return his greeting, so, too, will he not even look up if many rich men look upon him. For he knows that they differ not a whit from beggars . . . For men may all differ one from another, yet the wise man regards them as all alike because they are all equally foolish (*De constantia* 13.2, 5).

The person who would advance in philosophy must set aside all consideration of both the approval and contempt of the majority, who do not live by the same guiding principles. The philosopher is thus set free to live in accordance with the values of Stoicism and the behaviors and attitudes engendered by this philosophical subculture. Epictetus, a late first-century Stoic, also sets aside the censure of the non-philosopher as errant and, therefore, of no consequence. The lay person's opinion that the philosopher is vicious or foolish is comparable to the opinion that the day is not light nor the night dark—the outsiders' negative judgements condemn themselves (*Dissertations* 1.29.50–54).[20]

Second, honorable and dishonorable behavior must be redefined clearly in terms of the group's values, goals, and survival. The members are still motivated to pursue honor, and to act honorably in everything, but the group's values and beliefs define what constitutes honor. The pursuit of honor by the members of the group, therefore, leads to the cohesion and survival of the group. This carries the potential of conflict with other groups and with the representatives of the dominant culture. Wherever pursuits that are "honorable" in the group's eyes are seen as subversive or divisive by the larger culture, the latter will employ the means at its disposal to bring the "deviants" back in line with the dominant cultural values and allegiances. This scenario is at the heart of most every instance of "persecution" in the ancient world.

This is a prominent part of all minority cultural literature, whether the philosophical writings of the Greco-Roman world or the works of Jewish authors seeking to preserve the ethnic, cultural, and religious identity of their people. Ben Sira, for example, establishes obedience to Torah as the sole claim to being worthy of honor, the one factor which distinguishes people of worth from the dishonorable sort:

> What race is worthy of honor? The human race. What race is worthy of honor? Those who fear the Lord. What race is unworthy of honor? The human race. What race is unworthy of honor? Those who transgress the commandments . . . Those who fear the Lord are worthy of honor in his eyes. The rich, and the eminent, and the poor—their glory is the fear of the Lord. The nobleman, and the judge, and the ruler will be honored, but none of them is greater than the man who fears the Lord (10:19–24; RSV).

The criteria of honor within the dominant culture—wealth, political influence, and the like—are by-passed by Ben Sira, for such qualities would be attainable through assimilation to Greek culture, and the quest for success thus defined would certainly not preserve Jewish values

and identity. Therefore, honor and disgrace are now con-
strued specifically in terms of adherence to the values and
customs of the Jewish subculture: fulfillment of
φιλοτιμία, "love for honor," coincides with maintenance of the group boundaries and values.[21] Similarly, the
philosophical subcultures define the pathway to honor as
the set of attitudes and behaviors which fulfills the ideals
of the particular philosophy.

Thus, each member of the group is moved to seek
honor as honor is defined by the group's culture and values,
and to seek that honor and approval only from the other
members of the minority culture. This alternative "court of
reputation," often an overwhelming minority opinion, is
legitimized and fortified by the appeal to the "higher court"
of some divine or super-social force, which embodies and
enforces the values of the group and promises future vindication for the adherents of those values. Plato thus speaks of
living so as to achieve honor in the sight of God's court
(Plato, *Gorgias* 526D-527D), as does Epictetus: "When you
come into the presence of some prominent man, remember
that Another looks from above on what is taking place, and
that you must please Him rather than this man" (*Diss.*
1.30.1). This is a familiar device in the Jewish subcultural literature as well (cf. Sir 23:18–19).

Honor and shame language retains its prescriptive
and proscriptive force within the new definitions of the
honorable and disgraceful established by each minority
group. Those who seek to preserve the minority culture
use honor and shame language to direct the member to
seek distinction in the eyes of the higher court (reinforced, of course, by the group) and to disregard the evaluation of outsiders. When we turn to the Letter to the
Hebrews, we find all of these elements typical of a minority culture's use of honor and shame language. The
author seeks to desensitize the believers to the disgrace
and reproaches which they experience at the hands of the
dominant culture, developing at length the difference in

standards between what the society regards as honorable and what leads to honor before God. The author sets the believers before the court of God and the Son, who will bestow an eternal grant of honor on those who remain loyal to their obligations to the Divine Patron and the people of God. Persevering in living out the values of the minority culture will lead to greater and more lasting honor than success as the dominant culture defines it could ever bring. At the same time, violation (through disloyalty or ingratitude) of the patron-client bond formed with God through Jesus' ministry would bring down upon the Christian's head greater and more lasting disgrace than the society could ever heap upon the "deviants." Finally, the author grounds the believers' honor in a basis different from society's and untouchable by society, giving the community the theological resources by which to deflect the dominant culture's reproaches and contempt. He calls them to be sensitive only to their reputation before God and the community of faith throughout the ages, and not to fall into eternal disgrace for the sake of temporary honor in the world's eyes.

Dishonor and Disenchantment
The Situation of the Addressees

Many commentators have sought some pressing crisis behind the writing of Hebrews, as if some new, bloody persecution, or an imminent reversion to Judaism occasioned the letter. The author's response, however, leads us to consider another possible reason for the writing of Hebrews. The lingering effects of having been deprived of one's status and place within the society—having to go on facing the wearing experiences of rejection and dishonor because of one's commitment to the Christian minority culture—have led some to begin to separate themselves from the group. Some have begun to dissociate themselves from the Christian community, have backed off from their position of zeal, service, and witness, in order to be restored to honor and esteem in the eyes of their neighbors.

The Setting and Purpose of Hebrews in Scholarly Debate

Hebrews only reluctantly yields information about the circumstances which have arisen in the congregation and which arouse the author's concern. Scholars have therefore met with difficulty determining precisely what challenges the congregation faced and what the author hoped to effect by writing this letter. The sparse data which can be gleaned from the letter are gathered in the paragraphs below.

The congregation was founded by those who were witnesses to Jesus (2:3), and the reception of the gospel was accompanied by manifestations of God's power and presence (2:4) as well as by the first-hand experience of the Spirit (2:5). The author characterizes the congregation's earliest period as one of charismatic experience of the divine through the preaching of the faith (6:4–5). They held to this faith with a firm conviction (3:14), and were subsequently instructed in the foundational teachings of the Christian culture ("repentance from dead works, faith toward God, baptisms, laying on of hands, resurrection of the dead, and eternal judgement," 6:1–2). They actively showed love to the "saints," and performed "works" of service which God would not overlook (6:10).

The community's confession brought them into a time of conflict with the larger society. While this did not lead to the deaths of the believers (12:4), they "endured a severe contest of sufferings" (10:32). Some of the congregation were subject to reproach and their trials were made a public spectacle, and others demonstrated solidarity with those who were so treated (10:33), even with those in prison (10:34). Some also suffered the seizure of their property, as a result either of an official decree or of looting and pillaging while the owners were in prison, exiled, or otherwise occupied (10:34). The author attests to their willingness to suffer these things, however, on account of the hope and confidence they had (10:34–35).

At the time of writing, however, the character of the community has changed—so much so that the author has to remind them of what confidence and faith they once displayed, and what access to God and God's power they once enjoyed. They are in danger of "drifting away" (2:1) from the message that they received, of "neglecting" the message spoken by Jesus and attested by God (2:3), of "failing to attain" the promised rest (4:1), of falling through unbelief in the same way as the wilderness generation (4:12), of growing weary and losing heart (12:3). Even more strongly, they are in danger of falling into worse punishment than the transgressors of the Mosaic Law through "trampling underfoot the Son of God, regarding as profane the blood by which you are sanctified, and affronting the Spirit of favor" (10:29). Some have apparently begun to withdraw from the congregation (10:25), many have not lived up to what is expected from mature believers (5:12), and there appears to be a general faltering in commitment (e.g., 10:35–36, "Do not cast away your confidence," and 12:12, "Strengthen the weak knees and lift up the drooping hands").

What brought about this change? The letter is not explicit about this point. Some readers argue that the reference in 12:4, "you have not yet resisted to the point of blood," contains a shadowy implication of growing hostility against the believers and a coming persecution which the believers wish to avoid.[1] Others hold that the author's reliance on argumentation from the Hebrew Scriptures and his comparison of Jesus and the angels (who, in Jewish tradition, served as God's intermediaries when the Law was given to Israel), Moses, and the Jewish priesthood indicate that a strategic conversion back to Judaism (which enjoyed a measure of toleration within the empire which Christianity did not) was a lively possibility.[2] Both of these data, however, may point to purely rhetorical strategies of the author rather than reflect the nature of the occasion of Hebrews. Other scholars present a less dramatic picture, arguing that "moral lethargy" is the dominant problem that lies behind the epistle.[3] A number of scholars prefer to allow a number of factors stand side by side, understanding the author to respond here to one concern and there to another: "from the response that he gives to the problem, it would appear that the author conceives of the threat to the community in two broad but

interrelated categories, external pressure or 'persecution'
. . . and a waning commitment to the community's confessed faith."[4]

Viewing Hebrews against the cultural background of
a society which takes as its pivotal values honor and shame
leads to a new insight into both the nature of the "external
pressure" sensed by many scholars and the cause of the
"waning commitment" to Christian confession and involve-
ment. Such an approach leads beyond the stereotyped
picture of Christians being rounded up for execution in
the arena, or denying Christ before the emperor's tribunal in order to save their lives, to a more highly nuanced
sense of the pressures faced by early Christians in maintaining their confession and commitments to one
another, and of the ways in which they might have suc-
cumbed to those pressures.

The Community's Experience of Dishonor

Those who committed themselves to Christianity inher-
ited Judaism's restrictions on participation in the
Greco-Roman world. On account of their exclusive devotion to the One God and the accompanying refusal to
acknowledge any other deity, most Christians avoided
any setting in which they would be exposed to idolatrous
ceremonies. Since some form of religious worship formed
a part of almost every political, business, and social enter-
prise in the Greco-Roman world,[5] Christians adopted a
lifestyle which, in the eyes of their pagan neighbors,
would have been considered anti-social and even subversive. Loyalty to the gods, expressed in pious attendance at
sacrifices and the like, was viewed as a symbol for loyalty
to the state, authorities, friends, and family. By abstaining
from the former, Christians (like the Jews) were regarded
with suspicion as potential violators of the laws and

subversive elements within the empire. The Christians were subjected to prejudice, rumor, insult, and slander, and were even made the targets of pogroms and local legal actions. It was thus both dishonoring and dangerous to be associated with the name of "Christian."

The member of Greco-Roman society who sought honor and a good reputation achieved these goals largely through fulfilling the central values of that society—piety and benefaction. Piety involved not only demonstrations of reverence for the gods, but also included dutifulness towards state, laws, friends, and family. Worship of the deities was something of a symbol for one's dedication to the relationships which kept society stable and prosperous. The use of one's goods, influence, and the like to benefit others (thus establishing patron-client relationships) or to benefit one's city or country—was such an important path to honor that φιλοτιμία, "love of honor," came to be used almost as a synonym for "generosity."[6] Other members of society could be suspicious of those who did not honor the gods—the one who did not acknowledge the claim of the gods on one's life and service could not be counted on to honor the claims of state, law, family, and the traditional values of the society.

What appears to us as a religious claim, such as "Christ is Lord," was actually charged with political significance.[7] Greco-Roman polytheism was tolerant of foreign divinities, seeking to link the deities native to the provinces with the traditional Greek and Roman gods. Denial of the gods, however, was to deny the order of society, and was perceived as such a significant threat to social order and cohesion that this "atheism" was often punished with death. When we read, therefore, of Paul's injunctions to avoid all interaction with idols (e.g. 1 Cor 10:14–22; 2 Cor 6:14–7:1; 1 Thess 1:9), we should realize that such a course of action would bring the community into conflict with the larger society. How did their pagan neighbors view the Christian counterculture? How did they respond to those who formerly supported their society's values and deities, but had now turned aside from the "right" way? They employed the means of social control at their disposal to bring these deviants back into line with the dominant cultural values, using the negative sanction of disgrace and shame.

If we turn to the writings of non-Christian authors who have left evaluations of the Christian movement, namely Tacitus, Pliny, Lucian, and Celsus, we find that a strong social stigma was attached to those who joined the Christian communities. The historian Tacitus mentions the movement only in the context of Nero's scapegoating of Roman Christians for the great fire of 64 CE (*Annals* 15.44). The leader of the group (Christ) is remembered only as an executed criminal; his followers are slandered as lovers of every foul vice (the usual way to stigmatize a deviant group). Their religion he degrades as a *superstitio*, a derogatory term reserved for foreign cults (opposed to the respectful term *religio*).[8] In sum, the presence of a Christian community in Rome was regarded as one more example of "things horrible or shameful" from around the world breaking out in the imperial capital. Tacitus declares that the Christians suffered under Nero not so much for arson as for *odium humani generis*, "the hatred of the human race." This phrase may be taken to mean that the Christians were hated by the larger society, that their withdrawal from the normal civic, social, and political activities (on account of the practices of idolatry at these gatherings) indicated that the Christians were misanthropic, or as deliberately ambiguous and suggestive of two-way hostility. In either case, Tacitus shows that this particular sect stood in a high degree of tension with the society, and was regarded as a shameful and subversive presence in the empire.

Showing oneself dutiful toward the gods and religious traditions led to an honorable reputation in both the Greco-Roman and Jewish cultures.[9] The fruit of public piety is the attainment of a reputation for being a reverent, honorable, and reliable citizen. When the Christian withdrew from all participation in the traditional forms of piety and religion, he or she was deprived of this means of gaining honor and approval, attaining rather disgrace and hostility. Another minority culture in the Greco- Roman world which came under attack for its "atheism" was the Epicurean school of philosophy. The Greek author Plutarch, responding to this school, provides evidence for the widespread belief that piety and preservation of the state were inextricably linked—belief in the Greco-Roman gods was the bedrock of a stable society. Atheism threatened political anarchy and the subversion of the state (Cf. *Reply to Colotes* 31 [*Moralia* 1125D-E]).

The shameful reputation which attached itself to the name of "Christian," as attested by Tacitus, appears also in the famous letter of Pliny the Younger (*Letters* 10.96), imperial legate to Bithynia and Pontus in 110 AD, and is mirrored in a text written from the Christian side of this tension, namely 1 Pet 4:14–16: "If you are reproached for the name of Christ, you are enviable, because the Spirit of God's honor rests upon you. By no means let any of you suffer as a murderer, or thief, or evildoer, or a troublesome meddler; but if as a Christian, do not feel ashamed." In this text we find that society has applied its sanction of disgrace in order to bring its former adherents back into line, and that the representative of the minority culture ("Peter") has set aside the opinion of society and reinterpreted the experience of dishonor as a sign of honor before God.

The second-century critic Celsus reveals that similar slanders (vice, low-breeding) persisted into the second century, but also introduces another element: Christians do not support the government of the state. They do not "take office in the government of the country," which is "required for the maintenance of the laws and the support of religion."[10] Origen freely admits the truth of this charge. The mandate to avoid the idolatrous rituals which

surrounded much of political life (and the social networking involved in performing one's civic duties) stood
behind Christians' reluctance to pursue such offices.
Nevertheless, in the eyes of their non-Christian neighbors, such avoidance compounded the feeling that
Christians were apathetic, if not hostile, toward the common good. Because of this same mandate, Christians
were less able to develop friendship networks and
patron-client relationships outside of the Christian
group. While this kept the group culture strong and
insulated, it also prevented them from cultivating the
resources which would have afforded some measure of
protection in times of focused social and political hostility against the community. The Christians thus suffered
lack of esteem as well as lack of protection.

The remarks about Christians in these pagan authors
reveals that being associated with the name of "Christian"
set one in the margins of Greco-Roman society. Being a
Christian, in the eyes of the society, prevented one's
attainment of honor and targeted one for dishonor and
insult. The recipients of Hebrews, moreover, certainly felt
the full force of society's negative sanctions. In the one
experience of the community most fully described by the
author, one finds that these Christians have suffered significant loss of status and dignity as a result of their confession. This passage is all the more significant given the
author's reticence in providing details about the community's history:

> But remember the former days in which, having been
> enlightened, you endured a hard contest with sufferings,
> in part being publicly exposed to reproaches and afflic-
> tions, in part having become partners of those being thus
> treated. For you both showed sympathy to the imprisoned
> and accepted the seizure of your property with joy, know-
> ing that you possessed better and lasting possessions
> (10:32–34, author's trans.).

We cannot know how long ago the events of the "former days" transpired. All that we can say is that this period of public rejection, humiliation, and dispossession belongs to the community's past, and that the author perceives that the community must recover the same dedication and endurance which they displayed then but lack now. This description, moreover, shows that what was chiefly at stake was the honor of the Christian community (both collective and individual).

The experience is described in terms of a public show: some portion of the Christian community was subjected to open reviling, being held up to ridicule and shame.[11] The term used to describe the experience evokes the image of the theatre (arena), where games, contests, and public punishments occurred.[12] The public imposition of disgrace constituted a device of social control, by which the society sought to dissuade the afflicted from continuing in, and others from joining, the Christian counterculture. The Christians were subjected to "reproach" and "affliction" (τοῦτο μὲν ὀνειδισμοῖς τε καὶ θλίψεσιν). The first term suggests verbal assaults on honor and character, an experience shared by many early Christian communities.[13] Shaming and reviling were the society's way of neutralizing the threat Christians posed to their view of the world and constellation of values and allegiances. The burning experience of humiliation and rejection was geared toward "shaming" the deviants into returning to their former convictions and obligations as members of the dominant culture.[14] Because the addressees had successfully resisted earlier attempts at social control, their own past endurance makes them the best examples for their emulation in the present.

The society added physical punishment to the verbal "correction," which meant not only the inflicting of physical pain but reinforced the degradation of the person. Cultural anthropologists and their students have noted the close connection between a person's honor and the

treatment of that person's body.[15] That such was the case
in the first-century Mediterranean world is demonstrated,
for example, in the way Philo of Alexandria speaks of the
physical punishment suffered by the Jews there as a "disgrace" or "insult." ὕβρις, usually translated "outrage" or
"insult," is used also to refer to "assault and battery."
Exposed to verbal and physical attacks on their honor, the
recipients of Hebrews had been subjected to what has
been called a "status-degradation ritual,"[16] by which a
society neutralizes the threat posed by deviants to the
absolute and ultimate character of that society's values
and social arrangements.

Another noteworthy aspect of this experience was the
solidarity shown by those who had escaped being singled
out for this public punishment with those who were subjected to public humiliation, who thus voluntarily became
"partners with those thus treated," that is, partners with
the disgraced. This manifested itself in the care shown by
the community to those members who were imprisoned.
Prisoners in the Greco-Roman world relied on family and
friends from the outside to provide even the most basic of
needs (food, clothing, medicine). Lucian of Samosata, a
second-century CE writer of satirical prose, provides a
moving (if somewhat mocking) description of the
resources a Christian group would mobilize for one of its
own (*On the Death of Peregrinus* 12–13). The community
brought food, changes of clothing, bribes to the officers
for special treatment, and kept the prisoner company,
cheering him day and night. What Lucian describes in fic-
tion can be seen in truth from Ignatius of Antioch's journey to execution at Rome. The apostle Paul, who was
frequently in prison, similarly received gifts and encouragement from his communities.[17] Rather than be concerned for what the unbelieving society would think of
those who identified with such criminal deviants, the
believers consistently supported and maintained their

bonds with their sisters and brothers in prison or suffering society's other "correctional" procedures.[18]

A final component of the addressees' experience
alluded to by our author is the confiscation of the believers' property. The Greek term used refers most often to
plundering, the looting to which abandoned properties
often fell victim.[19] Even an officially sanctioned act, however, could be regarded as "plundering" by those suffering the loss.[20] It is also difficult to assess from this passing
reference what sort of property was taken. A court or local
official might have ordered the seizure of land and house,
or simply the imposition of a fine; unofficial plundering
(while the believers were involved in trials or imprison-
ments) would involve the loss of movable property, but
might nevertheless represent a substantial loss of wealth.
"Plundering" could also indicate driving people from
their homes in the context of a riot or pogrom.[21]

Whether the loss of property was occasioned by official or unofficial seizure, the loss of material wealth translates into a loss of honor and status. Inhabitants of the
ancient world did not accumulate wealth and possessions
for the sake of ownership or pleasure, but bartered material wealth for prestige and honor either through display
at private banquets or through benefaction. When one
lost material goods, one also lost the raw materials for
building prestige. Jerome Neyrey has argued that such
considerations applied not only to the wealthy landowner,
but even to the peasant in a village.[22] Such loss would further provoke contempt from others if the victim had
brought the loss on himself or herself.[23] This would have
been the case for the Christians in Heb 10:32–34:
through their own neglect of their obligations to society,
state, and gods, they had justly earned their misfortune.

This loss of property could also have put the believers
in an uncomfortable economic position. The Alexandrian
Jews (Philo, *In Flacc.* 57) lost their houses and workshops
in the course of the pogroms against them, with the result

that they were at once impoverished but also removed from access to the very tools of their trade and their shops by which they could again gain economic stability. The recipients of Hebrews may have suffered similar losses, and have found themselves in a lower economic status with no means of recovery. Further, as part of a disgraced "subversive" culture, they could not expect to regain the security of wealth through partnerships with non-Christian partners or benefactors.

In summary, the former experience of the community to which the author calls attention was one of humiliation, rejection, and marginalization. The Christians lost their place and standing in the society, stripped of their reputation for being reliable citizens on account of their commitment to an alternate system of values, religious practices, and social relationships. While the society intended this experience to draw the deviants back into line with the dominant culture, the believers remained steadfast in their loyalty toward God and the group, not allowing society's means of social control to deflect them from their faith.

The Community's Response to Dishonor

The author presents the incidents described above as exemplary precisely because the believers "accepted" these losses "with joy." While they had met these challenges boldly in the faith (10:35), the situation has changed. Those who were formerly bold and energetic in Christian witness and solidarity have become "sluggish" (6:12). Some are already in the habit of neglecting the group's meetings (10:25). The believers are in danger of "drifting away" (2:1), "neglecting so great a salvation" (2:3), having "unbelieving hearts" (3:12), "falling through such disobedience as the [wilderness generation's]" (4:11), "wavering in the confession of our hope" (10:23), being numbered among "those who have spurned the Son of God, profaned the blood of the covenant by which they were sanctified, and outraged the Spirit of grace" (10:29; NRSV), of "growing weary and losing heart" (12:3), and of "selling [one's] birthright" for short-lived temporal benefits (12:16). They are given the titles belonging to the heirs of the promise by the author, but can only keep them if they "hold firm the confidence and pride that belong to hope" (3:6), hold their "first confidence firm to the end" (3:14), and find the necessary "endurance" (10:36).

The situation thus presented appears to be a crisis not of impending persecution, nor of heretical subversion, but rather a crisis of commitment. The believers have experienced the loss of property and status in the host society without yet receiving the promised rewards of the sect, and so are growing disillusioned with the sect's promise to provide. As time passes without improvement, they begin to feel the inward pressure for their society's affirmation and approval. The fervor and certainty of their earlier life in Christ has cooled with their prolonged exposure to the pagan witnesses of their degradation, who no doubt continued to disparage the believers and regard them as subversive and shameful.[24] They have begun to be concerned for their reputation before society. Though they were able to resist it at the outset, the machinery of social control is in the long run wearing down the deviants' resistance. While they could accept their loss in the fervor of religious solidarity, living with their loss has proven difficult. The author writes as if apostasy is a lively option for the addressees: "How can we escape if we neglect so great a salvation?" (2:3; NRSV); "Take care, brothers and sisters, that none of you may have an evil, unbelieving heart that turns away (ἀποστῆναι) from the living God! (3:12; NRSV); "For it is impossible to restore those who . . . have fallen away" (6:4–6); "How much worse punishment . . . will be deserved by those who have trampled upon the Son of

God, regarded as profane the blood of the covenant . . . and outraged the Spirit of grace?" (10:29; NRSV).

Not the threat of violent persecution, nor a new attraction to Judaism, motivates this apostasy, but rather the more pedestrian inability to live within the lower status that Christian associations had forced upon them, the less-than-dramatic (yet potent) desire once more to enjoy the goods and esteem of their society. In the eyes of society, and perhaps increasingly in the eyes of some believers, renouncing that "confession" which had first alienated them from the dominant culture might be accepted as a step towards "recovery." We shall explore through the remainder of this study how it is precisely such a situation to which Hebrews provides a strategic response.

The Author's Strategy for Reshaping the Response

The author encounters his audience at this point of wavering, and challenges them with the claim that the real loss is not the deprivation of their place in society, but the forfeiture of their inheritance from God. They risk losing the lasting honor which God grants them if they "shrink back" under pressure from society:

> Do not throw away your confidence, which has a great reward. For you have need of endurance in order that, having done the will of God, you may receive the promise. For yet "but a little while" and "the one who is coming will come and not delay: and my righteous one will live by faith, and if he or she shrinks back, my soul has no pleasure in that one." But we are not characterized by shrinking back unto destruction but by faith unto the attainment of life (10:35–39; author's trans.).

The endurance of disgrace in the eyes of society has earned for the believers honor before God. Their commitment to Christ, their benefactor, through times of heavy social pressure will not go unrewarded. He urges them to understand their experience of marginalization as their obedience to God's will. They must continue in their "confidence" if they are to claim the promised "greater and lasting possessions" (10:34) and "glory" (2:10). Παρρησία, usually translated as "confidence," carries more the sense of boldness, candor, and openness. In this period, it often appears as the antonym for αἰσχύνη, or shame.[25] Refusal of the returning feeling of "shame" before society, and a firm grasp on the certainty of God's promises, will lead the believers to attain greater honor than they could ever enjoy at society's hands.

To achieve this goal, the author embarks upon a remarkably intricate and comprehensive argument. He seeks to detach the addressees from their concern for the opinion of non-Christians, thus separating them from the evaluation of those who seek to maintain not the group's but society's values and orientations. This he does by holding up before them as exemplary and praiseworthy the heroes of faith who have "despised shame" (cf. 12:2). A large segment of the concluding exhortation (10:32–12:3) is held together by this common theme: the community, Abraham, Moses, the martyrs, and Jesus all set aside the opinion of the unbelieving society and embrace a lower status in their eyes in order to maintain their commitment to God, the community of faith, and the promises.

He calls, them, rather to seek honor and fear disgrace only before the court of God (the higher "court of reputation"). He urges them to fulfill their obligation to their divine patron and benefactor, and not to return insult for the gifts they have obtained from God through Christ. Such an affront would result in an eternal ascription of dishonor at the Judgement. By remaining faithful (note the centrality of the virtue of "faith" in this letter, cf. 3:7–4:11 and 10:32–12:3), the Christians will indeed receive the promise of the inheritance of children of God, and enjoy the full honor of "partners of Christ" (3:14).

The author reinterprets their experiences of dishonor as signs of honor before God, and spurs them on to pursue the reward of "glory" (2:10) by continuing to live out the values and commitments of the Christian counterculture.

3
Despising Shame
Negating Society's Social Control

We recall from chapter one that encomia, or epideictic speeches which praises some figure or figures from the past, were intended to strengthen the commitment of the audience to the values embodied in those figures. Hearing others praised, they would be stirred to emulation of the behaviors which led to such esteem in the hopes of augmenting their own honor in the eyes of their group. Within deliberative speeches, ancient orators would often include shorter epideictic sections expressing the honor achieved in the past by those who embrace a course of action similar to that promoted by the speaker. So it is with the Letter to the Hebrews. The author is vitally concerned with renewing the addressees' commitment to the value of πίστις, which is generally translated as "faith." He argues that the way for them to attain the inheritance God has promised them is through remaining loyal to their patron and benefactor, God (10:36–39):

> You have need of endurance in order that, having done the will of God, you may receive the promise . . . For yet "but a little while" and "the one who is coming will come and not delay: and my righteous one will live by faith, and if he or she shrinks back, my soul has no pleasure in that one." But we are not characterized by shrinking back unto destruction but by faith unto the attainment of life (author's trans.).

The opposite course of action is also mentioned in these verses, namely ὑποστολή, a "shrinking back" in commitment to Christ. This appears as a concern throughout the epistle. The author therefore fortifies his exhortation by including an encomium declaring the honor and approval before God's eyes attained by the exemplars of commitment (πίστις) known to the community from the tradition of the Septuagint (the Greek translation of the Hebrew Bible, together with the Apocrypha) in order to stir up their waning zeal for honor before God and to reinforce the detachment of Christians from society's honor rating.

The chief models the author holds up for emulation in 10:32–12:3—the community, Abraham, Moses, the martyrs, and Jesus—all share a common feature. They have chosen to embrace a lower status in the eyes of the society in order to pursue the greater and lasting honor to be won through obedience to God. Renouncing the honor and approval which accompany success and integration into the unbelieving society, they have all borne witness to a hope for something greater—the eternal benefaction promised by God—and, in their loyal obedience to this hope have accepted marginality with regard to human networks of honor and status.

Jesus, the "Perfecter of Faith"

The climax of the author's encomium on "faith" is the example of Jesus in 12:1–3. All the heroes of faith in chapter 11 are in view here as the group of spectators to the race (and therefore a sort of "court of reputation" which will evaluate the runners) which the addressees are called to run, a race which Jesus has run before and successfully completed. As faith's pioneer, Jesus is the one on whom the addressees must fix their gaze; as faith's perfecter,[1] Jesus shows how faith achieves its goal. Jesus' faith manifested itself in that he "endured a cross, despising shame" (12:2); this same faith led to the honor which followed, when "he sat down at the right hand of God" (12:2). The phrase "despising shame" brings us to the heart of one of the main goals of the author, who seeks to detach his audience from placing value on society's approval or disapproval. Such concern for reputation in the eyes of non-group members, as we have seen, would pull believers away from the group and its values, and lead them to assimilate back into the dominant culture.

The recipients of Hebrews, who had embraced the loss of honor and status in order to remain loyal to God and Christ in the "former days," would certainly be sensitive to the loss of honor and status which Jesus endured on their behalf in order to secure for them the promised benefits of children of God. For the author of Hebrews, Jesus' humiliation begins with the Incarnation. In 2:5–7, he applies Ps 8:4–6 to the ministry of Christ, arguing that the phrase "you made him a little lower than the angels, you crowned him with glory and honor" (ἠλάττωσας αὐτὸν βραχύ τι παρ᾽ ἀγγέλους, δόξῃ καὶ τιμῇ ἐστεφάνωσας αὐτόν, 2:7), which in the context of the psalm speaks of the place of humankind in creation, refers to two succeeding events in Jesus' life. He reads the βραχύ τι in the first phrase as an expression of time, separating a period of abasement from a later exaltation. This pattern appears also in the important Christ-hymn of Phil 2:6–11, where again a voluntary loss of status is followed by a greater exaltation.[2]

Christ's humiliation climaxes, again as in the Philippians hymn, in the crucifixion. The author speaks of the suffering of Jesus in 2:10, 18; 5:8, but only gives it the specific shape of a cross in 12:2, a death which occurs "outside the camp" (13:11), a place of dishonor and uncleanness. Closely connected with this death is ἀντιλογία. Generally translated "opposition" or "contradiction," this term recalls more specifically the insults and mocking which Jesus had to bear during his trial and death.[3] This aspect of the passion will resonate deeply with the addressees' own experience of "reproaches and sufferings" (10:32–34).

Death on the cross was, by both Jewish and Greco-Roman standards, an averting admonition rather than an inviting example. Crosses are now ornately decorated and prominently displayed in sacred settings: in the first century they were revolting sights, rendering unclean the space they occupied. In the eyes of the world, such an ignominious death was most to be feared and not even mentioned in polite company. A "noble death," particularly in service to one's country or clients, was viewed as a special benefit conferred by nature or God on the virtuous (Ps.-Isocrates *Ad Dem.* 43; Josephus, *BJ* 7.325–26). A shameful death, however, leaving only lasting disgrace with no possibility of redress, was a most revolting prospect: "it is not a fearful thing to die, but to die shamefully" (Epictetus, *Diss.* 2.1.13).

Death on a cross was associated with "the lower classes, i.e. slaves, violent criminals and the unruly elements in rebellious provinces."[4] Crucifixion was painfully public, the victim being nailed up as a model for the behaviors most especially to be avoided rather than imitated. "By the public display of a naked victim at a prominent place . . . crucifixion also represented his uttermost humiliation."[5] Jesus' crucifixion, in the public eye, effected the destruction of his honor and memory. For the author of Hebrews, however, this same death exemplifies the perfection of the virtue of faith, and the pattern which leads to the rewards of faith. Paradoxically, the path to honor before God entailed the despising of disgrace before human society.

"Despising Shame"

In the history of interpretation, the phrase "despising shame" has been read as Jesus "braving" or "facing up to" the experience of humiliation which the cross entailed,[6]

or as a Stoic disregard for the experience.[7] These readings fail to capture the full impact of the author's meaning. The only lexical parallel in the Greek literature
appears in an oration by Dio Chrysostom (*Or.* 7.139), in
which Dio blames the increasing number of adulteries
committed with persons of lower status on the "open
trampling of modesty" (τῆς αἰσχύνης ἐν κοινῷ
καταφρονουμένης). Dio uses the term αἰσχύνη to
denote "modesty," here more narrowly connected with
regard for society's sexual mores. In a broader sense, it
affords a suitable parallel to Heb 12:2. In both, a sense of
shame, as regard for the values and opinion of society, has
been set aside. The author of Hebrews, of course, does not
recommend "despising shame" in the sense of violating
the strict sexual ethics of the Christian group (13:4), but
only in the sense of not allowing regard for unbelievers'
opinion of oneself to deter one from remaining faithful to
Christ and the community.

A similar phrase appears in Plutarch's *Life of Cato the
Younger*, in which this devotee of philosophy is said to
train himself to "be ashamed only of what was truly
shameful, and to ignore men's low opinion of other
things" (τῶν δ' ἄλλως ἀδόξων καταφρονεῖν). Cato
thus displays a certain independence from the society's
definitions of honor and shame and its use of sanctions to
enforce these definitions, preferring to take his bearings
from his philosophy rather than succumbing to social
pressures to adopt or abstain from certain behaviors.

Against this background, the phrase αἰσχύνης
καταφρονήσας takes on a more precise and socially formative shape. "Shame" (αἰσχύνη) here goes beyond the
experience of disgrace; it signifies sensitivity to the evaluation of one's actions and commitments by others.[8] When
one "despises shame," one sets aside concern for one's
reputation, and simultaneously places a negative value on
the opinion of those who would judge one's actions as disgraceful. This corresponds to the philosopher's setting

aside of the evaluation non-philosophers formed of his or her values, goals, and behavior. The person unacquainted with the truth was like a child, whose opinion counted for nothing (Aristotle, *Rh.* 2.6.14–15; Seneca, *Constant.* 13.2). Those who were dedicated to different ideals belonged in two different courts of reputation, which did not intersect.

The phrase indicates Jesus' awareness that the society which held him in contempt was unaware of what was truly valuable and honorable in God's sight, and therefore their evaluation of him simply did not affect his true honor in the least—a conviction confirmed by his subsequent exaltation to God's right hand. This was also the way the early church fathers read Heb 12:2. Jesus, as "lord of glory" was in a position to despise the opinion unenlightened human beings held of him (Origen, *Fragmenta in Psalmos* 37.12.4–5; Gregory of Nyssa, *Contra Eunomium* 3.5). Moreover, these early interpreters clearly perceive this detail of Hebrews' description of Christ's faith as an explicit model for the believers.[9] In his *Exhortatio ad Marytrium* (37.11–14), written in the period of the Decian persecution, Origen encourages the Christians to resist both social and physical pressures placed on them by holding up Jesus, as presented in Heb 12:2, as an exemplum: "Jesus then endured a cross, having despised shame, and on account of this sat down at God's right hand: and those who imitate him, despising shame, will sit with him and reign with him in the heavens."[10] John Chrysostom, commenting on this verse, also interprets Jesus' stance as a rejection of the opinion of unbelievers, and, as such, a model for Chrysostom's hearers. By accepting a shameful death Jesus taught his followers "to count as nothing the opinion of human beings.[11]

The author thus confronts the addressees, who were increasingly uncomfortable with the lower status they had fallen to on account of their commitment to Christ, and in whom a sense of "shame" with regard to the opinion of unbelievers was beginning to return, with the example of

Jesus. Jesus shows "faith"—the virtue which leads to God's approval (10:38–39) in its most complete expression. Faith rejects of the opinion of those who do not share the hope of the Christian, and considers valueless society's evaluation of those acts which obedience to God required; the believers are called to imitate this faith, in order that they may attain the promised reward and continue in their commitment to one another and to their divine Benefactor.

"For the joy that was set before him"

Jesus was able to disregard society's opinion and persevere in obedience to God because he looked to the reward which accompanies such obedience. Society is not in possession of all the facts, as it were, and so its judgements and evaluations are unreliable and unsound. The end result of honor before God vindicates the one who chooses obedience to God even if it entails disgrace before society. Hebrews thus encourages the readers to take their bearings also from the perspective of the heavenly reward, from which vantage point their experiences of dishonor are transformed into a noble contest for an honorable prize. The preposition ἀντὶ which introduces the second half of 12:2 offers an ambiguity caused by its multiple meanings. It has been taken to mean "in place of the joy set before him," signifying that Jesus, who was able "to rid himself of all annoyance and live a life of happiness and abundance of all good things, yet did he of his own free will undergo a death painful and replete with ignominy."[12] The preposition has also been interpreted as signifying "for the sake of," that is, "in order to obtain."[13]

The most informative parallel for solving this ambiguity appears in Aristotle's *Nicomachean Ethics* (3.1.7), which speaks of praise accruing to the one who submits "to some disgrace or pain as the price of some great and noble object" (ἀντὶ μεγάλων καὶ καλῶν). He adds that engaging in some disgraceful activity for a trivial motive (e.g., monetary gain) is entirely contemptible. Aristotle here claims that a noble goal and result can redeem as praiseworthy and honorable the one who has suffered some disgrace. The author of Hebrews, seeking to hold up as exemplary behavior one who suffered the greatest disgrace, provides here the lofty goal on the basis of which Jesus' honor is reestablished. The unbelieving society would continue to regard Jesus as a disgraced criminal, but before the court of God Jesus holds the highest honor: his session at God's right hand proves that he remained above reproach, and that he had in fact acted honorably.

Throughout the oration, the author has spoken of the benefits of Jesus' death. In so doing, he has affirmed that it was in fact an honorable death. He fixes this in the minds of the audience long before he mentions the disgrace which that death entailed in society's eyes. *Rhetorica ad Herennium* (3.7.14) indicates that a person's death, if it brought benefit to others, was considered a most honorable death.[14] The author of Hebrews points to Jesus' death as a manifestation of God's favor (χάρις), a tasting of death on behalf of all (χάριτι θεοῦ ὑπὲρ παντὸς γεύσηται θανάτου, 2:9). Jesus' death frees his followers from slavery to the fear of death (2:14–15). Since freedom was held to be "the greatest of blessings, while slavery is the most shameful and wretched of states" (Dio *Or.* 14.1), the liberation from slavery provided by Christ was a considerable benefaction.[15] Through suffering death, Jesus became the "cause of eternal salvation for all who obey him" (5:9). The cause of benefits was regarded as "something honourable and divine" (Aristotle, *Eth. Nic.* 1.12.8), such that the way of disgrace and suffering constituted a claim to great honor. Jesus' endurance of the cross is the prerequisite for Jesus' followers attaining the honor of God's children (2:10). The greatest benefit Jesus gained for his followers (or, his clients, to use the language of patronage) by means of his death on the cross was the cleansing of their conscience and the consequent gift of access to God's throne as a throne of grace (χάρις). Jesus' death enables his followers to stand before God in confidence and expectation (4:16; NRSV): "Let us therefore approach the throne of grace (χάρις) with boldness, so that we may receive mercy and find grace (χάρις)) to help in time of need."[16]

Jesus' death on the cross brought him greater honor before God than disgrace before human society. His endurance of the cross was the perfection of his training in faith and obedience: "Although he was a son, he learned obedience through what he suffered; and having been made perfect (τελειωθείς), became a source of eternal salvation . . ." (5:8–9; NRSV). Many scholars have devoted articles and monographs to interpreting the meaning of "perfection" in Hebrews.[17] One may perhaps most profitably compare Hebrews' use of the term with Wisd 4:10–13, where "becoming perfect" (τελειωθείς, 4:13) parallels "becoming pleasing to God (εὐάρεστος θεῷ γενόμενος, 4:10), which is the goal shared by the author of Hebrews: "for without faith it is impossible to please God" (11:6). This same faith which Jesus pioneered and perfected is the virtue the believers are called to emulate. Jesus' crucifixion, though shameful in the eyes of society, is an honorable course in God's sight, perfecting his approval before God, qualifying him for his ministry as high priest, and winning for him his exaltation to the place of highest honor, the seat at God's right hand (12:2).

Jesus, the exemplar of faith *par excellence*, enacts his faith by choosing the course of action that fulfills obedience to God without regard for the approval or disapproval of society: this is the meaning of "despising shame." Faith looks only to God's approval, seeks honor only as recognized by God's court.[18] Faith therefore remains steadfast in the face of society's attempts to pressure the believer into conforming to its values. Jesus' exaltation, moreover, proves the rule by exemplifying the extreme: the most revolting and degrading death in the world's eyes leads to the most exalted status in God's eyes.[19] The path of faith remains the way of honor, no matter what opinion society has of, or what dishonor society shows, the believers. Ultimately, God will vindicate God's clients before the eyes of the unbelieving world, when God shall "put all things under [Christ's] feet" (2:8; cf. 1:13; 10:13). On that Day, God shall rule the court of human opinion out of order and overturn its former verdicts.

The Witnesses of Faith

Jesus stands as the culmination of a series of examples of faith: the famous litany in praise of faith in Hebrews 11. The principles of selection at work in the author's construction of this encomium are too complex to be reduced to one motive or intent. One clear thread which links the more fully developed examples (i.e., Abraham and the Patriarchs, Moses, and the miscellany of the martyrs and marginalized) together, however, is that these figures embraced a lower status in the world's eyes for the sake of the heavenly reward. That is, they, too, "despise shame." Together with Jesus, these are the examples of those who "through faith and patience inherit the promises," whom the addressees are called to emulate (6:11–12).

The author reveals some important presuppositions of interest to our study concerning the meaning of "faith" in this epistle. First, faith looks to God as a Benefactor. The author writes that "without faith it is impossible to please God, for whoever would approach him must believe [that is, trust] that he exists and that he rewards those who seek him" (11:6). Faith acts so as to procure some promised benefit from God ("reward," 10:35; 11:26), and seeks to attach itself to God above all other potential benefactors (cf. Moses' choice of God's patronage to the exclusion of Pharaoh's favor, 11:24). Faith thus

pursues a patron-client relationship with the most powerful patron possible, and as such seeks to secure the honor
of both patron and clients. The divine Patron may be
called upon to vindicate the clients' honor, a perquisite
well attested by the Hebrew Scriptures (written within an
awareness of a covenant establishing this patron-client
relationship): "On God rests my deliverance and my
honor" (Ps 61:8 LXX). The client bases his or her claim
on previous evidence of fidelity: "Take away from me
their scorn and contempt, for I have kept thy testimo-
nies." (Ps 118:22 LXX). Fidelity and obedience to the
divine Patron provide assurance that the patron will preserve the client's honor.

Second, faith navigates its course by the unseen and
future realities, rather than taking its bearings merely
from the visible and present world. The exemplars of
faith are enabled to make the right choices because of this
wider vision (11:3, 7, 10, 16, 20, 22, 26b, 27b, 35b).[20] This
expanded scope relativizes the value of this present,
mutable world, and neutralizes the opinion of those who
make value judgements based on the partial vision of
looking to this world.[21] Access to this larger picture alone
enables the person of faith to endure the loss of status and
prestige which the actions of faith bring in the eyes of
unbelievers, and so attain life and honor before God and
in the memory of the community of believers.

Third, faith leads to μαρτυρία, "attestation" (11:2,
4, 5), gaining for the faithful a lasting testimony to their
worth and virtue. This term is used to speak of the
endorsement given by Roman authorities of a person
whom a local assembly wished to honor. The "witness"
borne by these authorities was to the worthiness of the
recipient of honors.[22] This sense carries over into the New
Testament, where this word can carry the sense of "bearing favorable testimony" and thus "spreading a good reputation."[23] The author creates an *inclusio* around the
whole chapter, using forms of μαρτυρεῖσθαι in the

opening verses of the litany of faith and again at the transition from encomium to hortatory peroration (11:39), indicating that the author wishes to underscore the similar attestation by the highest Authority of the worthiness of Christ's faithful clients.

Abraham and the Patriarchs

The aspects of Abraham's story which the author of Hebrews chooses to highlight are significant. The particular events and conditions selected reveal an interest in this patriarch which differs from Paul's, and which provides a description of faith again quite different from that of the apostle to the Gentiles:

> By faith Abraham obeyed when he was called to go out to a place which he was to receive as an inheritance; and he went out, not knowing where he was to go. By faith he sojourned in the land of promise, as in a foreign land, living in tents with Isaac and Jacob, heirs with him of the same promise. For he looked forward to the city which has foundations, whose builder and maker is God. By faith Sarah herself received power to conceive, even when she was past the age, since she considered him faithful who had promised. Therefore from one man, and him as good as dead, were born descendants as many as the stars of heaven and as the innumerable grains of sand by the seashore.
>
> These all died in faith, not having received what was promised, but having seen it and greeted it from afar, and having acknowledged that they were strangers and exiles on the earth. For people who speak thus make it clear that they are seeking a homeland. If they had been thinking of that land from which they had gone out, they would have had opportunity to return. But as it is, they desire a better country, that is, a heavenly one. Therefore God is not ashamed to be called their God, for he has prepared for them a city.
>
> By faith Abraham, when he was tested, offered up Isaac, and he who had received the promises was ready to

offer up his only son, of whom it was said, "Through Isaac shall your descendants be named." He considered that God was able to raise men even from the dead; hence, figuratively speaking, he did receive him back (11:8–19; RSV).

Whereas Paul sought Abraham's faith in his firm conviction that God would fulfill his promise to give him offspring (cf. Gal 3:15–18; Rom 4:13–21), here the emphasis is on his departure from his native land in obedience to God's call (11:8–10). This element of the patriarchs' faith is disproportionately highlighted in 11:13–16—is their confession to be "strangers and exiles on the earth" bears witness to the city of God and wins them association with God (11:16).

In the Greco-Roman world, one's native land was the source of one's sense of identity and belonging. The fellow inhabitants of one's native country or city formed one's group of significant others, one's primary reference group.[24] Living away from one's native land, moreover, resulted in a loss of the status enjoyed in that native land (particularly that which came from the honor developed by the family over generations). This state of affairs was aggravated by limited access to acquiring honor in the foreign land. Indeed, sojourning was considered a state of humiliation (so Lucian, *My Native Land* 8), and the terms "exile," "foreigner," and "immigrant" (τὸν ξένον καὶ τὸν μέτοικον) could be used as insults (Plutarch, *De exilio* 17 [*Moralia* 607 A]). The stranger or foreigner is usually barred from enfranchisement in the new location. Lacking citizenship and the rights and protection it afforded left one defenseless against insult, abuse, and assaults on property or honor.[25] Citizenship provided some measure of security, a comfortable "mooring" within society: lack of citizenship left one adrift.

The choice by Abraham and his family to embrace the life of "strangers and foreigners" (ξένοι καὶ παρεπίδημοί, 11:13) would therefore have been heard by the addressees as a choice of a lower status liable to dishonor and danger, undertaken for the sake of obedience to God's call.[26] The author has focused the recipients' attention on this aspect of Abraham's faith because it answers most nearly the condition of the letter's recipients (cf. 10:32–34). While they had not physically moved from their native land, their rejection at the hands of their neighbors—expressed in the abuse and insult directed toward them—signifies their social dislocation. They had lost their former status and the dignity and security that status afforded them. The patriarchs are further praised in that they chose not to return to their native land, and to the political safety and security which that would bring, choosing rather to press on in their quest for a "better homeland, that is, a heavenly one" (11:16). This again mirrors the addressees' situation, who must choose between renouncing Christ (and thus regaining society's favor) and remaining exiles in their society for the sake of enrollment in the "city which is to come" (13:14).

Just as the heavenly city founded by God carries greater value than earthly cities founded by human beings, so it confers on its citizens greater prestige than the citizens of earthly cities. The people of God strive for honor in the heavenly city with the same vigor displayed by those seeking the fleeting honor of the transient cities of the world. Commitment to God, or "faith," manifests itself precisely in refusing to call any city in this world their home. In this regard, Dio's claim (*Or.* 44.6) before his native city is informative. Having lived in exile for many years, he avoided acquiring citizenship or land abroad in order to demonstrate his loyalty to his native Prusa, a dedication which he expects will win him greater approval and honor there where he most desires it. In the same way, the patriarchs' refusal of earthly citizenship assures them of honor and approval—indeed, high civic standing—in the city which God has established and will reveal. This grant of honor is expressed in God's willingness to have the divine Name associated with them (11:16). By this, God reveals their true worth (they are worthy to be associated with God) and pledges to preserve their honor as an extension of God's own honor.[27]

In leaving their native land in obedience to God, Abraham and the patriarchs embraced the lower status of foreigner, sojourner, and stranger and the exposure to reproach and dishonor which attended this change of status. They confessed this status and persevered in it (11:13, 16), despite the fact that the option to return to their former status in their native land remained a possibility (11:15). They remain unaffected by any sense of shame before the worldly court of opinion, such that they are not moved to return from their marginal relationship with society to a place of honor in society's eyes. Rather, they seek only the honor of a better citizenship before God and God's approval, which they receive in the form of association with God's name (11:16).

Moses

The second well-developed example of faith in Hebrews 11 is Moses. The author again formulates his description of Moses' faith to answer the situation of his addressees.

> By faith Moses, when he was grown up, refused to be called the son of Pharaoh's daughter, choosing rather to share ill-treatment with the people of God than to enjoy the fleeting pleasures of sin. He considered abuse suffered for the Christ greater wealth than the treasures of Egypt, for he looked to the reward. By faith he left Egypt, not being afraid of the anger of the king; for he endured as seeing him who is invisible. (11:24–27, RSV)

The author focuses not upon Moses' part in giving the Law—rather, central to Moses' faith is his renunciation of status and honor in the sight of the world and his adoption of the degraded status of the slave in order to bind himself to the people of God and share in their future enjoyment of God's benefactions. This pattern matches the community's past choices (10:33–34) and is called for in the community's present (13:3).

Moses' first act of faith appears in his refusal "to be called a son of a daughter of Pharaoh" (11:24). A member of the royal family of Egypt, even regarded as the heir of Egypt's throne by Philo and Josephus,[28] Moses enjoyed exceptionally high status and honor. If Moses would have been content to remain the grandson of Pharaoh, and thus enjoying Pharaoh's patronage, he would have enjoyed the prestige and power of a king, as well as access to the "treasures of Egypt," which would have placed in Moses' hands the means to gain great honor as a benefactor. By faith, Moses renounces such status and promise of honor, and rejects Pharaoh's patronage. He exchanges his inheritance in Pharaoh's court for the inheritance of the slave, disdaining the honor offered by human courts of reputation.[29]

Moses chooses, rather, "maltreatment together with the people of God," and joins himself to slaves, people of no honor in society's eyes, and thus subject to insult and physical outrage. The pleasure he refused, however, is qualified in two important ways. First, it is merely πρόσκαιρος, "temporary." This adjective stands in stark contrast to μένων, "abiding," which the author frequently uses to describe the inheritance of the faithful (10:34; 12:27; 13:14). The honor and security this temporary enjoyment of worldly status and wealth bestows has no lasting value. Moreover, it will become a liability in the future, when God comes to judge the world. Temporary pleasure will yield to lasting pain and disgrace, because this "pleasure" is in fact ἁμαρτία, "sin." "Sin" here signifies something more specific than a transgression of one of God's commands: it is the rejection of living in solidarity with the people of God.[30] Sin in Hebrews means the renunciation of fellowship with the people of God for the sake of a return to peace and favor in the unbelieving world. Sin is precisely the "shrinking back" which the author warns against (10:38–39), the attempt to avoid

further "ill-treatment with the people of God" for the sake
of honor as Christ's enemies define it and bestow it.
Moses' faith expresses itself in the choice for loss of status
and safety in the world.

Moses is able to make this choice because he properly
evaluates the value of the "reproach of Christ" to be
greater than the "treasures of Egypt" (11:26), for his eyes
are firmly fixed on the reward (11:26b). Here again, faith
evaluates worldly realities in light of the eternal, and this
broader perspective reveals that what brings temporary
reproach and dishonor before the world's court actually
leads on to lasting honor before God's court. The phrase,
"the reproach of Christ" (τὸν ὀνειδισμὸν τοῦ
Χριστοῦ), which has its roots in Psalm 88:51–52, connects Heb 11:24–26 with 13:12–13, which exhorts the
addressees to choose to bear Christ's reproach also: "So
Jesus also suffered outside the gate in order to sanctify the
people through his own blood. Therefore let us go forth
to him outside the camp, bearing his reproach (τὸν
ὀνειδισμὸν αὐτοῦ φέροντες)." Moses' experience,
moreover, recalls the addressees' former experience of
disgrace endured because of their loyalty to Christ.
There too (10:33) one finds mention of reproaches
(ὀνειδισμοί) resulting from being associated with the
name of Christ, and which was the common possession of
many Christian communities (cf. 1 Pet 4:14–16; Matt
5:11; Luke 6:22).

What Hebrews means to signify by "the reproach of
Christ" is thus perhaps best illuminated by Ps 69:8, 10: "it
is for thy sake that I have borne reproach, that shame has
covered my face . . . For zeal for thy house has consumed
me, and the insults of those who insult thee have fallen on
me" (NRSV). Those who insult God pour out their scorn
also on God's servants. Nevertheless, just as Jesus set aside
the disgrace ascribed by unbelievers and embraced the
reproach which accompanies obedience to God, so Moses
did, and so the addressees are called to do. The "reproach

of Christ" thus signifies the abuse incurred through persisting in the same obedience to God's call as Jesus exemplifies, as well as the hope that those who have thus shared in Christ's sufferings will also share in the exaltation and reward which Christ received (cf. 12:2; 2:10).

Moses, like Christ and Abraham, also "despises shame." He renounced the worldly honors which were his to pursue by birth (or, technically, adoption) and, as Jesus (cf. Phil 2:5–11), left the prestige of a throne to assume the lot of a slave. He chose to join himself to God's people and their destiny, even though it entailed dishonor in the world, rather than to enjoy adulation and pleasure in the society of unbelievers, at the cost of being joined with them in everlasting disgrace. Knowledge of God's reward relativizes both the sting of temporary disgrace and the incentive to pursue worldly honors, allowing Moses, like Abraham, to leave his native land (11:27) and join the people of God in their pilgrimage toward the promised reward. Hearing the praise of Moses, the addressees are called to embrace the loss of their own place in society, and to choose to continue in solidarity with the people of God through their assembling for worship (10:25) and their service to their marginalized brothers and sisters (13:3).

The Martyrs and Marginalized

As he concludes the praise of heroes of faith from the pre-Christian era, the author moves from a summary of those who performed mighty and miraculous works by faith to an account of those who were tortured, killed, or otherwise disenfranchised for their commitment to God and perseverance in fulfilling the requirements of faithful clients:

> Some were tortured, refusing to accept release, that they might rise again to a better life. Others suffered mocking and scourging, and even chains and imprisonment. They were stoned, they were sawn in two, they were killed with the sword; they went about in skins of sheep

and goats, destitute, afflicted, ill-treated—of whom the world was not worthy—wandering over deserts and mountains, and in dens and caves of the earth (11:35–38, RSV).

The author joins these to the summary of kings, warriors, and charismatic prophets in order to show that what matters is commitment to God, not the honor or dishonor of the circumstances in which that commitment is expressed. Those who were "tortured to death, refusing to be released," seem to the world to have been defeated, but in God's sight they are no less victorious and praiseworthy than those who "through faith conquered kingdoms" or "became mighty in war."

The first figures among this group—those who were tortured to death for the sake of a better resurrection—are the martyrs who suffered under Antiochus IV,[31] who served as examples of commitment to God and Torah in Hellenistic Judaism. Indeed, their exemplary role intrudes upon the very narrative of their sufferings (cf. 2 Macc 6:28, 31), and their story is taken up again by the author of 4 Maccabees as the noblest examples of those who died on behalf of virtue (1:8), motivating hearers to "obey the law and exercise piety in every way" (18:1).

The martyrs' experience of being tortured to death—like Jesus' own crucifixion—involved not only subjection to the extremity of physical pain, but also involved complete degradation. The physical violation of the person entailed an assault on the person's honor, who was denied any possibility for the reparation of his or her honor in this life. Pain and shame were intentionally joined (cf. Heb 12:2), as seen in the mocking, scornful atmosphere of the torture of the seven brothers (2 Macc 7:7, 10). Like Jesus, they endure the pain and do not allow the experience of disgrace to weaken their commitment to God and their resolve to remain obedient. Hebrews makes it clear that they had a way out, indeed a way back into ease and honor: like Abraham, they had the opportunity to abandon the journey—to be "released." Like the other exemplars of faith, however, the martyrs persevered in order to obtain the reward, here described as "a better resurrection."[32] They refuse (indeed, despise) Antiochus's promises of high status (cf. 2 Macc 7:24; 4 Macc 8:5–7), knowing that their obedience to God will bring them greater and more lasting honor and security before God. Thus the martyrs repeat Moses' choice, spurning the offer of a patron-client relationship with a worldly regent in order to preserve inviolate their status as God's clients (and the benefits that will bring).

The martyrs do not share in the definitions of honor held by Antiochus, the non-Jews, and the Hellenizing Jews. These consider it to be of the highest value to advance in Greek culture, acquire Greek citizenship, and become a part of the ruling elite within the dominant culture. The martyrs, however, hold it to be honorable to preserve obedience to Torah and keep themselves from sin or pollution (cf. 2 Macc 6:19–20, 28). In the eyes of the Hellenizers they appear to be acting irrationally and dishonorably, spurning the good; in their own eyes (and, they assure themselves, in God's eyes) resistance and endurance of disgraceful treatment preserves their integrity and honor. The martyrs seek honor and recognition, however, not from the court of the Gentiles, but from the court of God and the community of faith (4 Macc 13:17; 17:5, 20).

The Maccabean martyrs are joined by an unnumbered host of those who suffered a variety of martyrdoms, physical abuse, and forms of social dislocation for their commitment to God (11:36–38). The author uses the rhetorical device of accumulation to create a picture of a flock of faithful ones who are marginalized in the extreme, enjoying no place in society, subject to every form of disgrace at society's hands. Disgrace is explicitly the lot of those who "suffered mocking," and implicitly for the scourged, imprisoned (cf. the experience of some believers in 10:34 and 13:3), and executed—all marks of society's disapproval and rejection. Those who went about homeless, lacking the shelter indicative of any place in civilization, were also subject to the opprobrium of the world, as the inability to provide for one's needs brings disgrace in that society. This again connects with the experience of at least some in the community who had been deprived of their property and thus, depending on the extent of this confiscation, of their protection from penury.[33] The details added by the author concerning the clothing of some members of this group of witnesses points explicitly to their social location—they dress not in the accoutrements of civilization, but rather of voluntary exile in the wilderness.[34] Indeed, the author's description of these exemplars as "wandering," and his location of them not in centers of society like cities, towns, or even farms, but rather in the "deserts, mountains, caves, and holes in the ground," signifies their opposition to the social order and their rejection of society.[35] This is the stance to which the author hopes to win the addressees, as he will later exhort them to "leave the camp" (in terms of any sense of belonging or ambition, rather than physical removal, 13:12–14).

In the middle of this list of those who are dishonored by society's standards, the author introduces a striking remark. His claim that "the world was not worthy of them" (11:38) encapsulates the reversal of evaluations of honor and disgrace which undergirds the author's exhortation. Here again he turns the norms of society upside-down, affirming that the faithful person's true worth is not measured by the standards of the Greco-Roman society. On the contrary, it is the society that will be measured by the standard of the faithful. The author of Hebrews thus effects a coup similar to that of Epictetus in his discourse on the Cynic, in which the Cynic (a word etymologically akin to "dog") becomes the one who evaluates worth and the standard by which others are assessed.[36] The world's rejection and negative evaluation of the faithful is in fact a judgement upon the world.[37] Only those who obey God, who secure God as their Patron, who look also to the unseen and future realities when evaluating and making choices are capable of knowing what is truly honorable or shameful: it is their critique of the unbelievers which is valid, not the opposite.[38] *Sub specie aeternitatis*, their sufferings become "noble" (cf. 4 Macc 11:12), and what constitutes a "shameful death" in the limited vision of the Hellenizers is transformed into a "blessed death," and therefore a "noble death" (4 Macc 12:1).

The martyrs and the marginalized of 11:35–38 thus also "despise shame." Spurning the honors offered by the unbelieving society at the price of conformity to its norms and expectations, they choose to endure temporary disgrace and degradation and so hope to preserve their honor before God and attain God's promised benefits. They reject the ill-founded standards by which the world arrives at its unreliable evaluations of what is honorable and shameful. Like Jesus, they set aside all sensitivity to the approbation or opprobrium of the world, and so are freed to pursue approval before God's court. The addressees are urged to have the same faith.

The Example of the Community

The author strategically prefaces these examples of despising society's negative evaluations for the sake of a positive evaluation by God with the use of the addressees themselves as exemplars of faith in 10:32–34. The author urges them simply to persevere in their former laudable course, so as not to fall short of the reward which their past actions have already all but won for them. Orators would frequently appeal to a group's past accomplishments or investment in a particular endeavor in order to encourage the completion of a task begun. For example, at the climax of Tacitus's *Agricola* (33–34), the Roman general rallies his troops with these words:

The long road we have traveled, the forests we have
threaded our way through, the estuaries we have
crossed—all redound to our credit and honor as long as we
keep our eyes to the front . . . I would quote the examples of
other armies to encourage you. As things are, you need only
recall your own battle-honors, only question your own eyes.[39]

The rhetorical appeal is based on *pathos* as much as *logos*.
The orator motivates his hearers first by rousing confidence. Just as the army (here) succeeded in its former
endeavors, which were not unlike the present challenge,
so it would succeed again. This device also works by rousing fear—the army's former achievements and honor are
in fact in danger of being marred by failure to act and persevere in the present. Dio provides a second concise
example of the linking of ambition and fear in his para-
phrase of *Philoctetes* (*Or.* 59.2): "This thirst for glory
(φιλοτιμία) leads me to . . . accept every fresh peril, fear-
ing to mar the glory won by earlier achievements."[40] The
author of Hebrews thus harnesses the double-edged spur
of this device, drawing the addressees' attention to their
former endurance and faithful action, intensifying its
power by pointing out the proximity of the goal
(10:35–36).[41] It is a mark of honor for them to continue in,
and a mark of dishonor to abandon, their former course.

We have seen that the "great contest" to which the
author directs the readers' attention involved disgrace
and loss of status, and the addressees are praised precisely
for enduring dishonor (10:32). They are being chal-
lenged to continue to endure society's attacks upon their
honor, resisting the temptation to "shrink back" in the
face of society's opposition from the course which faith
requires, namely perseverance in the confession of Christ
and solidarity with those who belonged to Christ. When
threatened with the loss of their property, the markers of
their status and place in society, they accepted such loss
"with joy," placing value only on their "better and lasting
possessions" (10:34).[42]

The author urges the addressees to continue to manifest such παρρησία—which clearly signifies here more than "openness" or even "confidence". As it is elsewhere an antonym of αἰσχύνη (Phil 1:20; 1 John 2:28), so here it would be well to read it as the opposite of sensitivity to society's opinion. The community had been "bold" in the face of society's disapproval and its sanctions of reproach and punishment. They are called to continue in that "boldness" so that they may receive God's reward, and not fall into the company of those who "shrink back" and lose God's approval (10:38). Written in the community's own past endurance is the faith of Abraham, who relinquished his status in his homeland in order to attain new status as a citizen of God's city, and the faith of Moses, who chose disgrace and maltreatment in solidarity with God's people over ease and honor apart from them. They are thus encouraged to persevere in their former faith and commitment (πίστις), and assured that, if they do, they will exchange their temporary dishonor in the sight of the world for eternal honor before God.[43]

Conclusion

The author of Hebrews seeks to rouse emulation and imitation through the praise of the exemplars of πίστις, particularly those who have "despised shame." Sensing that the addressees are becoming sensitive once again to society's opinion of their worth, and becoming ambitious to regain their lost status in their neighbors' eyes, the author seeks to direct their attention back toward the alternate arena of honor where so many have successfully competed and attained a lasting praiseworthy remembrance before God. He hopes to spur them on to complete their race for honor before that court, while insulating them from society's means of enforcing adherence to its self-preserving values and goals—that is, by reinforcing their ability to "despise shame." He thus sets them on a course toward continued hostility with the host society (cf. the earlier experiences of 10:32–34) which may even lead to the loss of life (12:4).[44]

Such a course, however, leads to solidarity with Jesus and the replication of his faith.[45] Jesus' honor in the unseen, eternal realm will inspire his followers to endure as he did, despising shame.[46] By such a path of *imitatio Christi*, the addressees will attain the κρεῖττόν τι, the "something greater" which God has prepared for them (11:39–40). Christ's own achievement of honor (the "joy set before him," τῆς προκειμένης αὐτῷ χαρᾶς, 12:2) will motivate the addressees to persevere in the "contest set before us" (τὸν προκείμενον ἡμῖν ἀγῶνα, 12:1), the prize of which is a share in Christ's own honor (μέτοχοι τοῦ Χριστοῦ, 3:14).[47] The value of such a prize transforms dishonor before the society (the attendant circumstances of faith) into esteem before God and the community.[48] Πίστις, which in Hebrews combines "faith" in the reality and beneficence of God as well as commitment to persevere in answer to God's call, leads to future reward and honor. The author of Hebrews thus shares the basic conviction of Jews and Christians that those trusting in God will not fall into lasting disgrace, but rather rise to great honor.[49]

Seneca (*Constant.* 19.2–3) writes that sensitivity to insult adversely affects one's performance in society, leading one to "refuse to face both public and private duties." Hebrews addresses a situation with a similar danger: if the addressees reawaken to sensitivity with regard to society's opinion of them, and to society's use of dishonor as a negative sanction, they will fail to persevere in faith and its works, and so fail to achieve the eternal honor God has prepared for them.

The author has selected and fashioned his examples of faith in order to remedy this dawning problem and to provide positive models for their imitation, assuring them that lasting honor attends the faithful. First, the

community's own history provides the best model for
their future, replicating as it does the pattern of the
heroes of "faith." The believers have lost their place in
their homeland for the sake of God's promise, and, like
Abraham, are not to grow weary and turn back from their
pilgrimage in order to regain that lost status. Rather, they
are to press forward in faith toward the land of promise,
leaving behind the unbelieving world: "let us go forth to
[Jesus] outside the camp and bear the abuse he endured,"
seeking "the city which is to come" (13:12–14).[49] Like the
martyrs, they are not to seek to reduce the tension
between themselves and the dominant culture because of
their commitment to God. They are urged rather to continue to devote themselves to the community of believers,
assembling together for mutual support (10:25) and caring for those who have been particularly singled out by
society for punishment (13:3). Like Moses, they are to
choose solidarity with the people of God, even at the cost
of exclusion from the pleasurable enjoyments of honor
and wealth which society offers to its faithful.

4
Honor, Gratitude, and the Divine Patron

While Hebrews seeks to move the addressees to "despise shame" by many positive models of those who have scorned society's estimation of them for the sake of achieving honor in God's sight, it also goads them in that direction through a fearsome presentation of the alternative—despising or slighting God. Within the argument of Hebrews, one either honors and obeys God at the risk of dishonoring and provoking the world, or one honors and conforms to society at the risk of dishonoring and provoking God. Stated another way, one either seeks to gain security through adopting the representatives of the unbelieving society as one's patrons, or one attaches oneself to God and enjoys the benefits gained through Christ.

Hebrews' Christology, central to the history of investigation, comes forcefully into play at this point. The author develops the superior dignity of Christ in order to direct the addressees' attention to two crucial points: first, he appeals to the virtue of justice, which insists that the believers return the proper honor to the One who occupies a place of supreme status in the Jewish-Christian cosmos; second, the author appeals to the obligation of gratitude, since Jesus has made use of his exalted position for the benefit of his clients, securing God's favor and benefaction ($\chi\acute{\alpha}\rho\iota\varsigma$) as their mediator. Negatively, the author strongly cautions his audience against doing that which would dishonor the Son and, through Him, God, thus turning favor into wrath, breaking off the patronage of God in favor of judgement.

Here the author is still using concerns of honor and dishonor to drive his exhortation, but now it is not the addresses' sense of their own honor that is in view, but rather their concern for the honor due to another and the consequences of failure in that regard.[1] Appeals to *pathos* (especially "fear" and "confidence") figure prominently in the author's demonstration of the honor due God and the danger which faces the one who chooses to dishonor Christ.

The Honor of Christ

The author adapts his presentation of Christ to the situation of the addressees, seeking to fix in the minds of his audience the supreme honor of Christ. He places two alternatives before his hearers: they may continue to know this exalted person as their benefactor and their means of access to an even greater Benefactor, or they may reject Christ as their benefactor, spurn his gifts, and incur the enmity of the One who upholds the honor of Christ, namely the Living God. The author develops Christ's superior honor by means of dwelling on the christological titles "Son" and "High Priest," and also through the christocentric reading of several psalms, which locate him in the place of highest standing in God's court.

The Honor of the Son

In the letter's *exordium*, or prologue, the author presents Jesus to his audience immediately as "Son," the bearer of the final word of God (Heb 1:1–2), specifically as the "Son of God" (1:5; cf. 4:14; 6:6; 10:29). The honor of Jesus is thereby established as embedded within, and protected by, the honor of God. That the child inherits the honor of the parents is amply demonstrated by Dio's claim to respect purely on account of his illustrious father and

grandfather (*Or.* 46.3–4), by the custom of introducing an
encomium (honorific speech) of a person with an account
of his or her parentage, and by the explicit statement of
Ben Sira 3:11: "a person's honor springs from the father's
honor, and a mother in dishonor is a cause of reproach to
her children."

The declaration of Jesus' sonship is first of all a claim
about Jesus' honor and dignity in the cosmos. One may
compare our author's interest in Jesus as "Son" with the
observation in 2 Pet 8:17 that God's declaration of Jesus'
sonship invested him with a grant of honor from God:
"having received honor and repute (τιμὴν καὶ δόξαν)
from God the Father when the voice was conveyed to him
by the Supreme Glory: 'This is my Son, my beloved, in
whom I am well pleased'." The declaration of affiliation
here, as in God's confession of the patriarchs in 11:16,
indicates God's investment of God's honor in the Son,
Jesus. The superior status of Jesus as "Son" is then developed through comparison with the angels (1:5–14) and
Moses, the "servant in God's house" (3:1–6). Jesus is the
"reflection" or "effulgence of God's glory (ἀπαύγασμα
τῆς δόξης)," that is, Jesus shines with the honor and status with which God has invested him.[2] The comparison
with Moses, like that with the angels and the Levitical
Priesthood, does not imply a polemical purpose: rather
the author builds up the honor of Jesus through the tech-
nique of *synkrisis*, "comparison," an essential part of
ancient encomia (cf. Aristotle, *Rh.* 1.9.38–39). The author
relies on Moses' high standing in Hellenistic Judaism (cf.
Sir 45:1–3) as the foundation for his claims about Jesus'
superior dignity.

Jesus' Standing in the Court of God

The author also demonstrates Jesus' honor when he
speaks of Jesus' placement in the court of God. In the
ancient world, relative dignity was reproduced in such

things as seating order at a feast (cf. Luke 14:7–11) or at a court (cf. Esth 1:14; 3:1), in physical gestures and salutations (e.g., bowing), and in rituals or symbols concerning some part of the body (e.g., crowning or anointing). Hebrews brings together all three physical signs of honor when speaking about the dignity of the Son.

First, applying Ps 100:1 to Jesus, the author speaks of Jesus as "seated at the right hand of God" (1:3; 8:1; 10:12; 12:2), thus occupying the place of highest honor in the Jewish-Christian cosmos. The image of session at God's right hand was calculated to "convey to contemporaries an impression of the Son's royal power and unparalleled glory."[3] Second, the author provides a number of images depicting Jesus' honor through physical gestures and actions. Malina and Neyrey, following Pitt-Rivers, note that "honor is displayed when the head is crowned, anointed, touched, or covered."[4] Again appealing to quotations from the psalms, Hebrews enhances Jesus' honor with the depiction of being crowned and anointed by God (1:9; 2:7–9). Furthermore, from his seat of honor at the right hand of God, Jesus awaits the subjection of all things under his feet (cf. the "not yet" in 2:8). Jesus' enemies, who oppose the Son rather than show the Son his due honor will be subdued: "Sit at my right hand, till I make thy enemies a stool for thy feet" (1:13, again citing Ps 110:1). The placement of enemies under the feet is another physical representation of relative status, and a sign of Christ's dominance. A similar gesture appears in the angels' *proskynēsis* (1:6), although there the homage is offered voluntarily. This day of complete subjection, like the day of Christ's final inheritance of "all things" (1:3), is still in the future: the addressees are thus called to align themselves under the banner of the Son who will share his future honor with his clients.

The Honor of the Greater High Priest

Hebrews is well known for its "high priestly Christology": the designation of Jesus as "high priest of our confession" (3:1; cf. 2:17; 4:14; and 6:20) is aimed at contributing to the addressees' appreciation of Jesus' honor as well as describing his activity within the Heavenly Sanctuary. The office of high priest carried with it great esteem. Josephus (*BJ* 4.164), for example, calls the title of "high priest" the "most honored of revered names," and speaks of the office as "the highest dignity" (*BJ* 4.149). Philo of Alexandria shares this high regard for the office (cf. *De Vita Mosis* 2.142), even claiming that "the law invests the priests with the dignity and honour that belongs to kings" (*De spec. leg.* 1.142). The special dignity of the high priest derives from his role as mediator of God's good will and benefits (an aspect of Hebrews to be explored at length in the following section).

Hebrews adds to the honor of Jesus as "Son" the honor of the office of "high priest." The same psalm which declares the former provides the evidence for the latter as well:

> One does not take the honor upon himself, but is called by God, just as Aaron was. So also Christ did not exalt himself to be made a high priest, but was appointed by him who said to him, "Thou art my Son, today I have begotten thee"; as he says also in another place, "Thou art a priest for ever, after the order of Melchizedek." (5:4–5; RSV)

Just as Aaron had received divine legitimization for his priesthood, so Jesus is no usurper of the title, but duly appointed by God. As comparison with Moses had given force to the superior dignity of the Son, so now an extended comparison between Jesus' priesthood and the Levitical priesthood serves the same end. Here, however, the author sets aside the Levitical order in the process of exalting Jesus' priesthood: Jesus provides the closer and regular access to God impossible under the

Levitical priesthood, and so leaves no place for the mediation effected by the latter. Nevertheless, the honor of
Christ as greater high priest is enhanced by the honor
which attaches to the priesthood he replaces (cf. Sir
45:6–7, 18–20, 23–24).

Jesus stands not in the Levitical order, but as a "priest
after the order of Melchizedek" (cf. Ps 110:4). This psalm
affords the author an opening to read the story of
Melchizedek's encounter with Abraham after the battle of
the kings as a demonstration of the superiority of the order
of Melchizedek over the order of Levi. Abraham, the illustrious ancestor of Levi, demonstrates Melchizedek's
greater dignity by giving him the tithe of the spoils and by
receiving the blessing of this mysterious priest (7:4–7).
Jesus' priestly order can therefore claim a more illustrious
founder that the Levitical order. Moreover, Abraham's
descendant Levi is also found to be inferior to the successor
of Melchizedek, namely Jesus.

The author proceeds throughout the central section
of Hebrews (7:11–10:18) to compare the Levitical priests,
the earthly sanctuary, and the sacrifices prescribed by
Torah with Jesus, the Heavenly Sanctuary, and the
once-for-all sacrifice of Jesus' own self. On every point,
the superiority of Jesus' priesthood is established, and
with it the superior dignity of the "high priest after the
order of Melchizedek."

The Son and God's Favor

Jesus' honor as Son of God and as High Priest after the
order of Melchizedek gives him a claim to the deepest
respect and reverence. Before the court of God, his honor
is acknowledged by the angels and symbolized in his session at the right hand of God, the seat of pre-eminence in
the Jewish-Christian cosmos. It is none other than God
who has conferred these honors upon Jesus, and so it is
the duty of the just person to give to Jesus what is his due,

lest he or she incur the indignation (νέμεσις) of the God who consumes the rebellious and disrespectful with the fire of his anger. The author stresses also, however, the benefits which may be enjoyed by those who continue in the course of action which honors the Son. Jesus' death, which was regarded as a disgrace by the unbelieving world (12:2), brought him the greatest honor, for it was his death that was the constitutive act of his priesthood—the offering of himself once-for-all (cf. 10:12, 14). Jesus' death became his initiation into the unique priesthood of Melchizedek, and that single sacrifice, the author claims, has an abiding effect. On the basis of that sacrifice, Jesus' priesthood brings access to the greatest of benefits for those who "draw near to God through him" (7:25).

Patronage in the Ancient Mediterranean World

The ancient Mediterranean world has been accurately described as a patronal society, in which the giving and receiving of benefactions was "the practice that constitutes the chief bond of human society" (Seneca, *De beneficiis* 1.4.2). This patronal society was supported by an infrastructure of networks of allegiance and favor, whether between equals (who called each other "friends," and for whom the dictum "friends possess all things in common" held true) or unequals (the patron-client relationship, where the language of friendship was, however, also commonly employed so as not to draw attention to the inferior status of the client).[5] R. P. Saller observes that "precise evaluation and exact repayment of debt was rarely possible in the realm of day-to-day social favors,"[6] such that the relationships were ongoing (because the accounts were never "balanced"). Mutual bonds of favor and indebtedness provided the glue which maintained social cohesion.[7] In such a society, gratitude would be an essential virtue, and ingratitude indeed the "cardinal social and political sin."[8]

Patrons gave access to goods, entertainment, and advancement. One who received such a benefit accepted the obligation to "publicize the favor and his gratitude for it," thus contributing to the patron's reputation.[9] The client also owed services to the patron, and could be called upon to perform most any task,[10] thus contributing to the patron's power. A third figure in this network of patronage has been called the "broker" a term introduced into the discussion by Jeremy Boissevain: "Persons who dispense first-order resources [e.g., land, jobs, and the like] may be called patrons. Those who dispense second-order resources [i.e., strategic contacts or access to patrons] are brokers."[11] One must imagine the same personal relationship and duty between broker and client as between patron and client. Indeed, the "broker" is not a third entity *sui generis*, but rather a "client [or friend] to a patron and . . . patron to a client."[12]

The institution of brokerage is exceedingly well documented in the letters of Pliny the Younger, Cicero, and Fronto.[13] Brokerage is an expectation among political figures. Sophocles (*Oed. Tyr.* 771–774) provides an early literary example of this in Creon's defense against Oedipus's charge of conspiracy to usurp the kingship:

> I am welcome everywhere; every man salutes me,
> And those who want your favor seek my ear,
> Since I know how to manage what they ask.

Creon enjoys the salutation of a patron, but his chief benefaction is access to Oedipus and favor from the king. Many of Pliny's letters to Trajan document the former's attempts to gain imperial *beneficia* for his own friends and clients. Particularly informative is *Epistulae* 10.4, in which Pliny seeks from Trajan the grant of senatorial office for Voconius Romanus. He addresses Trajan clearly as a client addressing his patron, and proceeds to ask a favor for

Romanus. Pliny's character is offered as a guarantee of his client's character, and Trajan's assessment of the second-hand client is inseparable from his assessment of Pliny—indeed, Trajan's "favorable judgement" of Pliny (not Romanus) is the basis for Trajan's granting of this favor (cf. also *Ep.* 10.5–7, 10).[14] The broker, or mediator, at the same time incurs a debt to his or her patron and increases his own honor through the indebtedness of his or her client. Brokerage occurs also between friends and associates in private life. A familiar example appear in Paul's letter to Philemon, in which the apostle seeks to gain forgiveness for Onesimus, appealing to his convert on the basis of friendship: "So if you consider me your partner (κοινωνόν), welcome him as you would welcome me" (Phlm 17; NRSV).

Jesus as Patron and Broker

Given the prevalence and embeddedness of the system of patronage in the Mediterranean world, it is fitting that Jesus should be regarded as the patron of the Christian community, another expression of a wider tendency to conceptualize human-divine relationships by means of the language of patronage, seen, for example, in traditional Roman religion and in the adoption of "patron deities" by individuals and collectives (e.g., guilds or cities).[15] The exalted status enjoyed by Jesus (developed at great length and detail through dwelling on Jesus' sonship, priestly status, and session at God's right hand), carries the promise of great benefaction and advantage for those who make themselves clients of the Son.

The author's language emphasizes the patronal role of Jesus: he "helps (ἐπιλαμβάνεται) the descendants of Abraham" (2:16) and comes "to the aid (βοηθῆσαι) of those who are tempted" (2:18). He is thus the one to whom Christians are to look to supply what is wanting in their own resources, which places him in the role of the Patron, who provided assistance in many forms to clients.

Christians, indeed, have been brought into God's household (3:6) through their clientage to the Son, thus under God's protection and provision.

The author speaks of Christ's death in terms of the numerous benefits this selfless act brings to those committed to Jesus, a fact which, we have seen, also develops the honor of Jesus. The greatest benefit of Christ's death for our author derives from Jesus' appointment as "high priest after the order of Melchizedek," through which "he became to all who obey him the cause of eternal salvation" (5:9). In this capacity, Jesus affords access to God. He is the broker, the mediator (μεσίτης, 8:6; 9:15; 12:24), who secures favor from God on behalf of those who have committed themselves to Jesus as client dependents.[16]

Jesus provides the second order resource of access to God as μισθαποδότης, "rewarder," allowing his clients, formerly separated from God by their sins, to approach God as their Patron rather than the Judge of those who have affronted God through disobedience (cf. 10:30–31). Access to God as Patron and protector was a familiar *topos* of philosophical literature. Epictetus (*Diss.* 4.1.91–98), for example, speaks of the search for the best patron under whose aegis to travel through life—one who could provide security against all assaults and in whom one could rely utterly not only for today but also tomorrow. His search leads finally and only to God: "Thus [the searcher] reflects and comes to the thought that, if he attach himself to God, he will pass through the world in safety."[17] Christianity, to use the expression of Barbara Levick, "gave access . . . through an incorruptible intermediary, to a reliable authority," an important offering indeed in a patronal society.[18] The discursive sections of Hebrews, which consist largely of comparisons between Jesus, the angels, Moses, and, centrally, the Levitical priesthood, seek to demonstrate the supreme efficacy of Jesus' brokerage of God's favor and his certain provision of access to the presence of the Divine Patron.

Jesus as Son—A Better Mediator than God's Servants

The emphasis placed by the author of Hebrews on Jesus' "Sonship" (cf. 1:1–6) has itself important implications for Jesus' efficacy as a mediator of God's *beneficia*. In his attempt to discover "who possessed *gratia*" in the Roman imperial world—that is, who was in a position to provide access to imperial *beneficia*—Saller points first to the imperial household: "When sons and grandsons existed, they and *their friends* were always natural candidates for the emperor's beneficence."[19] The close relatives of the emperor, especially his sons, were sought after as mediators of the emperor's favor. Their close, familial relationship to the patron of the empire gave great hope of success.[20] Thus when the author of Hebrews presents Jesus as "Son" in 1:2, and constructs his comparison of Jesus with the angels in 1:4–14, his aim appears to be to emphasize the greater proximity of Jesus to God as mediator of divine favor. The angels, also familiar to the first-century Judeans and Christians as mediator figures, are strictly a second order of brokers when compared to the Son.

G. E. M. de Ste. Croix notes that any member of a great person's extended household could serve as a broker of that great person's favor. The list includes "his friends, who had the ear of the great man; their friends, even, at only one further remove; even the personal slaves of the great man, who often, for the humble client, could procure or withhold audience with the patron—all these satellites shone with various degrees of reflected glory and were well worth courting."[21] Throughout Hebrews, one finds members of God's extended household at various degrees of remove, contrasted with Jesus, the Son. The angels are God's servants who are sent out to serve God's clients (i.e., "those who are about to inherit salvation," 1:14); Moses is a faithful, and hence trusted, servant in God's house (3:2). As a valued servant in the household, Moses would provide a certain level of access to the patron of the house, namely God. The author stresses, however, that the believers have gained the Son as their patron and broker of God's favor: their access to favor is assured by the mediation of the one who stands in such close proximity to God that he bears "the reflected radiance of God's glory" (1:3).

Jesus as Priest—The Efficacious Mediator

The heart of the letter (7:1–10:18) is devoted to a lengthy argument which stresses that the benefit of such access to God cannot be attained through the mediation (brokerage) of the Levitical Priesthood. As with the earlier comparisons with Moses and the angels, this comparison continues to enhance Jesus' honor, but is also specifically calculated to heighten the value of Jesus' mediation of divine favor for the community. Within the scriptural tradition and the practice of Second Temple Judaism, the Levitical priesthood figures prominently in its claim to broker access to God. The author therefore increases the value of Christ's mediation by showing the limitations and ineffectiveness of the only alternative sanctioned by scriptural tradition.

The author criticizes the Levitical priesthood because of the severe limitations it placed on access to God. This was demonstrated spatially in the layout of the tabernacle— the people remained in the outer courts, the priests could go only as far as the holy place, and the high priest alone enjoyed face-to-face access to the Divine Patron (9:1–3, 6–7). This access, however, was further limited temporally— on only one day out of the liturgical year could the high priest enter the Holy of Holies to engage in this face-to-face audience (9:7). The Levitical priesthood was unable to broaden access to God, for, our author argues, it could not take away the sins which stained the conscience and prevented the people from looking to God with confidence for benefaction (9:9; 10:1–4). The conscience (συνείδησις) bears an "internal witness" to the fact that "defilement extends to the heart and mind."[22] An imperfect conscience, mindful of the affronts given to God, cannot stand before God in expectation of a benefit, but only in expectation of judgement and wrath. "Perfection" of conscience entails a decisive purgation of sins, such that the breach in the divine-human relationship is sealed and the possibility of favor restored.[23] The offering for sin on Yom Kippur, far from removing the obstacle which stands in the way of forming a patron-client relationship with God, calls attention to the obstacle, providing only a reminder (ἀνάμνησις) of sins (10:3).

The author dwells on the failure of the Levitical priests in order to exalt Christ's success and stress the uniqueness of the benefit made available by him to those committing themselves to him. Hence, he underscores also the folly of relinquishing such an irreplaceable yet necessary gift by not continuing in loyalty and gratitude towards Christ. As Attridge comments, the author's "basic interest is to establish the significance of Christ for the present and future of his addressees by indicating the superiority of the Son to any other agent of God's purposes."[24] Christ alone is the effective broker of access to God as Benefactor. This gives Jesus a claim to the greatest honor, gratitude, and loyalty. Before Christ's ministry, one only had recourse to the ineffective priests established by the Law; his death has opened up unrestricted access to God following the perfection of the worshippers who draw near through Christ.

Jesus makes this available through his superior priestly mediation, or brokerage in matters divine. The author claims that Jesus has made the necessary purification for sins. Through the "sacrifice of himself" Jesus has decisively "put away sin" (9:26) and "obtained eternal redemption" (9:12; cf. also 1:3 and 2:17). Jesus' sacrifice, offered once for all (10:12), provides the cleansing of the conscience of the worshippers required, such that they might have confidence before God and assurance of divine favor (9:14). Again, this perfection indicates the removal of sin. The author explains "perfection" (10:14) by referring to the promise in Jeremiah 31 that "their sins and their lawless deeds I will remember no more" (10:17). This proves for the author that Jesus' sacrifice has effected the final purgation of sins which leaves neither remembrance of sins (before God or in the conscience of the worshipper). Jesus' sacrifice restores favor to the relationship of God and human beings, who now may stand before God as pleasing to God, and hence may stand in expectation of God's patronage.[25]

Jesus has, through the veil of his flesh (10:20), entered the Heavenly Sanctuary to stand perpetually before God as mediator "on our behalf" (9:24). Jesus' offering of himself makes him the "mediator of a new covenant," who fills this role precisely "in order that those who have been called may receive the promise of the eternal inheritance, since a death has occurred which redeems them from the transgressions under the first covenant" (9:15). The "promise" is a key term encapsulating the manifold benefactions gained through Jesus' brokerage.

Jesus does not, like the Levitical high priest, enter the sanctuary only once annually, but rather stands there continually, having passed into the true sanctuary of heaven. Further, he does not enter there on behalf of his clients who wait outside without access to God. Rather, Jesus' passage into the Heavenly Sanctuary opens up the way for believers to know and approach God as Benefactor and Patron.[26] Jesus has entered "as a forerunner for us" (6:20), as the author envisions the consummation of the Christian pilgrimage to be entrance into the rest of the city of God, the heavenly homeland (11:14; 13:14). Such final access, however, follows upon the access which can be enjoyed now in this life:

Since then we have a great high priest who has passed through the heavens, Jesus, the Son of God, let us hold fast our confession. For we have not a high priest who is unable to sympathize with our weaknesses, but one who in every respect has been tempted as we are, yet without sin. Let us then with confidence draw near to the throne of grace (τῷ θρόνῳ τῆς χάριτος), that we may receive mercy and find grace to help in time of need (ἵνα λάβωμεν ἔλεος καὶ χάριν εὕρωμεν εἰς εὔκαιρον βοήθειαν, 4:14–16; RSV cf. 10:19–22).

The mediation of Jesus allows his followers to draw near to God, looking to God as their benefactor. The "priestly" or "religious" tone of this central section of Hebrews should not obscure the fact that divine-human relationships are still being conceptualized in terms of patron-client relations. What is at stake is access to God's favor and benefits.

Χάρις **and Patronage**

A term of central importance for discourse about patronage is χάρις, which dominates an important transitional section of Hebrews, namely 4:14–16.[27] Heb 4:16 twice employs the noun χάρις, once to describe the "throne" (referring by metonymy to the One seated upon the throne), once to describe the expected result of such an approach. Usually translated as "grace," Classical and Hellenistic Greek authors place this word squarely within the social-semantic field of patronage and clientage. Aristotle, for example, defines χάρις as the disposition of a benefactor "to render a service to one who needs it" (Rh. 2.7.2). The word was used also to refer to the proper return for a benefit, namely gratitude, as in Dio, Or. 31.37: "For what is more sacred than honour or gratitude (χάριτος)?" Finally, it may refer to the actual gift or benefit conferred, as in 2 Cor 8:19 where Paul speaks of the "generous gift" he is administering (i.e., the collection for the church in Jerusalem). The claim of Malina and Rohrbaugh that, "in the New Testament, the language of grace is the language of patronage,"[28] is a quite welcome observation, placing the nebulous and indefinite term "grace" into a definite social and lexical province of meaning.[29]

Jesus' gift of access to God (4:14–16) affords the community access to resources for endurance in faith so that they may receive the benefactions promised for the future, to be awarded before God's court at the end of the age. The believers may draw near to God and expect to "receive mercy and find favor"—that is, the disposition of God to give assistance—"to help in time of need" (4:16). Such access would be expected to engender confidence in the believers, giving them a hopeful orientation toward the world.[30] Through Jesus, the believer has become a client of God, and may enjoy the confidence which accompanies the nearness of such help. In emphasizing this benefit won by Christ for his clients, the author has moved into the topic of Security, according to the author of the *Rhetorica ad Herennium* (3.2.3) the other component of "advantage" and goal of deliberative oratory (together with honor).

According to the author of Hebrews, the relationship of human beings with their God takes a decisive turn in the ministry of Jesus. Under the Old Covenant and its ineffective brokers of divine favor, the people stand in fear of God, and cannot approach to stand in God's presence. Under the New and Better Covenant, of which Christ is the Mediator (κρείττονος διαθήκης μεσίτης, 8:6), the believers find not fear but confidence to approach boldly, encouraged by the angels and souls of the righteous praising the Benefactor:

> For you have not come to what may be touched, a blazing fire, and darkness, and gloom, and a tempest, and the sound of a trumpet, and a voice whose words made the hearers entreat that no further messages be spoken to them. For they could not endure the order that was given, "If even a beast touches the mountain, it shall be stoned." Indeed, so terrifying was the sight that Moses said, "I

tremble with fear." But you have come to Mount Zion and to the city of the living God, the heavenly Jerusalem, and to innumerable angels in festal gathering, and to the assembly of the first-born who are enrolled in heaven, and to a judge who is God of all, and to the spirits of just men made perfect, and to Jesus, the mediator of a new covenant (διαθήκης νέας μεσίτη), and to the sprinkled blood that speaks more graciously than the blood of Abel (12:18–24).

Apart from Jesus, there is no such access to χάρις, such that the hearers are powerfully motivated to remain loyal to their Patron in order to retain the benefits of his brokerage. Schweizer's striking statement thus appears to have considerable merit: "the sacrifice on the cross opens to the new High Priest the way to heaven. Strictly speaking the cross is therefore not the saving event itself, but the act that makes the saving event possible."[31] The cross represents the sacrifice offered by the Mediator of the New Covenant, which is a part of the larger picture of Christ as priest, where Jesus' saving power is most clearly located for the author of Hebrews.

Jesus' death inaugurated the New Covenant, the goal of which is to cause "those who have been called" to receive the "promise of an eternal inheritance" (9:14). Those who exhibit faith and perseverance "inherit the promises" (6:12), which entails "salvation" (σωτηρία, 1:14), and "reward" (μισθαποδοσία, 10:35). The content of this future benefit includes the promise of honor and the possession of that which inspires respect, as Jesus leads the "many children to glory (πολλοὺς υἱοὺς εἰς δόξαν ἀγαγόντα)" (2:10). The believers hope for the "better and lasting possessions" (10:34) for which they willingly suffered the loss of their worldly possessions, and to which their faith gives them a "title-deed."[32] They will be given a place in the "rest" (κατάπαυσις) promised by God (4:8–9), citizenship in the city which God has prepared (11:16; 13:14) and a share in the "unshakable kingdom" (12:28).

The Proper Response to One's Benefactor

The author reminds his audience at length of the uniqueness and magnitude of Jesus' benefits in order to motivate them to make a proper response. This entails, first, the demonstration of respect for the Benefactor, acting in such a way as to enhance his honor—certainly avoiding any course of action which would bring him into dishonor, which would lead to the clients' exchanging favor for wrath, χάρις for ὀργή. Honor from those benefited was the return expected for patronage. Aristotle (*Eth. Nic.* 1163b1–5) states that "honour is the due reward of virtue and beneficence." One party would enjoy the benefit, the other the "prestige" which came from "the ability to confer services which were highly valued and could not be remunerated."[33] The client was expected to return honor not only in his or her own demeanor and actions, but in public testimony to the benefactor (cf. Seneca, *Ben.* 2.22.1; 2.24.2).

The second essential element of a proper response is gratitude, which signifies more than a subjective feeling. Seneca (*Ep. Mor.* 81.27) writes:

> No man can be grateful unless he has learned to scorn the things which drive the common herd to distraction; if you wish to make a return for a favour, you must be willing to go into exile, or to pour forth your blood, or to undergo poverty, or . . . even to let your very innocence be stained and exposed to shameful slanders.

Gratitude such as Seneca describes involves an intense loyalty to the person from whom one has received beneficence, such that one would place a greater value on service to the benefactor than on one's place in one's homeland, one's physical well-being, one's wealth, and one's reputation. The bond between client and patron, or, one should add, between friends who share mutual beneficence, is thus truly the strongest bond in Greco-Roman society. Where the sanctity of gratitude is maintained,[34] it becomes the one support which remains after all other values and valuables have crumbled—truly the cement of society which Seneca and others have claimed it to be. Such, the author of Hebrews claims, is the gratitude, the loyalty, which is due the Benefactor and Broker of God's favor, Jesus. When the author concludes his exhortation in 12:28, he stresses this second sense of χάρις: ἔχωμεν χάριν, "let us show gratitude." Saller notes that such *amicitia*, indeed whether between equals or unequals, "was supposed to be founded on virtue (especially *fides*)."[35] It is this *fides*, or πίστις, to which the author of Hebrews enjoins his readers through both negative and positive models, through warnings and exhortations.

The Danger of Violating the Bond of Patronage

The severity of the author's warnings stems from his perception that at least some believers are in danger of making an improper response, indeed of violating the sacred bond of the patron-client relationship. They are in danger of outraging the Son of God, of relinquishing their enjoyment of present benefits (e.g., access to God) and hope of future benefits (e.g., entering the promised rest) in favor of provoking God's anger, bringing upon their own heads God's satisfaction for the affronts to his honor. They are in danger of encountering God as Judge and Avenger, of receiving punishment, and hence disgrace, before his court at his coming, when every enemy will be subjected to Christ. Turning away from the discursive sections which develop the comparison of Jesus with other mediator figures in the Jewish tradition, we look now to the hortatory sections, in which the author expatiates on the ill consequences that will attend the violation of the patron-client bond through distrust and improper evaluation of the divine *beneficia*, and urges them through repeated warnings to consider the honor due their Benefactor.

The Pattern of Distrust—the Wilderness Generation

Πίστις appears as one of the more prominent virtues upheld and urged by the author of Hebrews (cf. 10:32–12:3). Πίστις forms a contrastive pair with ἀπιστία, which appears as the fatal flaw (coupled with ἀπείθεία) of the wilderness generation, developed in the author's first extended *exemplum* in 3:1–4:11. The importance of this early example derives from the later, extensive, and positive portrayal of the virtue of πίστις, for which the wilderness generation serves as a foil. The addressees are urged not to repeat the folly of their spiritual ancestors, who provoked their Benefactor to anger (3:10–11) through their distrust in God's good will and ability on the very eve of God's deliverance of the promised land into their possession. Here the author has in mind the events of Numbers 14: the echoes in the psalm of the events related in Exodus are muted in the LXX translation. While the MT of the psalm directs the reader to the complaints of the wilderness generation over the lack of water at Massah and Meribah (Exod 17:1–7 and Num 20:2–13), as well as the oath made by God in Num 14:21–23 in the wake of the rebellion, the LXX translates the Hebrew place names such that the whole passage now refers to Numbers 14, the peoples' refusal to take the land as God commanded on account of their fear of the inhabitants.

Despite God's continued provision from the deliverance from Egypt to the threshold of Canaan, the Israelites refused to go forward in faith. The πίστις word-group involves trust or reliability: in common Greek usage, πίστις refers both to the responsibility accepted by another to discharge some duty or provide some service and the affirmation of the reliability of that other in the person who awaits the fulfillment of the obligation.[36] Πιστός describes the person who may be relied upon to carry out the obligation, who is "trustworthy." Ἀπιστία may either signify the untrustworthiness of a base person or the feeling which ascribed unreliability to another, such that one neither entrusts that other with something nor trusts that other to fulfill an obligation.

A closer examination of the situation of the wilderness generation reveals the basic patron-client structure, and the fulfillment of obligations, underlying the narrative. God has undertaken an obligation to bring the people into the land which God promised to give them, and had provided many proofs of reliability (καὶ εἶδον τὰ ἔργα μου, Heb 3:9). In light of the spies' report concerning the might of the native inhabitants of the land, however, they wavered in their trust, that is, doubted whether or not God would be able to fulfill his obligation (Num 13:31–14:4). Indeed, they ascribe to their Patron the base motive of treachery—bringing them to this place to die (Num 14:3)—and abandon the prospects of the promise being fulfilled by setting in motion a plan to return to Egypt (Num 14:4), thus negating all the benefits God had already given them. Such distrust is interpreted by God as a test of God's reliability and ability to provide, which is nothing less than a challenge to the Benefactor, all the more inappropriate given the number of tests God had allowed in order to stimulate trust (πίστις).[37]

Distrust derives from a value judgement, specifically a low estimation of the honor and ability of the person whom one distrusts. Distrust is the proper response to base persons, οἱ πονηροί.[38] As such, the wilderness generation's response of ἀπιστία enacts a negative value judgement on God and insults their Patron, who alone is truly "good" (ἀγαθός). The Numbers narrative explicitly links distrust and the provocation which arises from contempt: "And the Lord said to Moses, 'How long will this people despise me? And how long will they not believe in me, in spite of all the signs which I have wrought among them?" (Num 14:11).[39] Insofar as they withdrew their trust from their Benefactor, they declared God to be unreliable and unable to fulfill the obligation God had assumed in their behalf; they declare God to be base, and so repay their proven Benefactor with flagrant contempt and disobedience, thereby rejecting the right and authority of the Patron to command obedience (an expected return for receiving benefits).

God's response is one of "wrath" or "anger" (Heb 3:10) towards those who have been disobedient, who have trampled the promise, and faltered in their trust. Anger, we recall from Aristotle (*Rh.* 2.2.1), is aroused in response to a violation of the honor to which one believes oneself entitled, particularly when affront comes from those "on whom they have conferred or are conferring benefits . . . and all those whom they desire, or did desire, to benefit" (*Rh.* 2.2.8). This well describes the situation in Numbers 14. God's every act in the narrative has been to bring the people from a wretched into an enviable state, leading them from slavery to a land for their own possession. Those whom he desired to benefit, however, returned insult for favor, slighting God through their distrust of God's good will and ability. The explicit expression of God's wrath is the people's irrevocable loss of access to the promised benefit through God's oath which excludes the rebellious generation from the promised land (3:11). The author ascribes this loss to disobedience and distrust (3:18–19; RSV): "And to whom did he swear that they should never enter his rest, but to those who were disobedient (τοῖς ἀπειθήσασιν)? So we see that they were unable to enter because of distrust (δι' ἀπιστίαν)." Their inability to recover favor is demonstrated in their abortive attempt to regain their inheritance (Num 14:40–45).

A secondary negative example of the impossibility of a return to favor, that is, to the hope of the benefits which were once spurned, appears in the author's recollection of Esau, who is permanently barred from his birthright once he trades it away (12:17). Esau has no regard for God's promises and benefactions, represented here by his birthright as a son of Isaac, the son of Abraham. His incorrect evaluation manifests "a decisive contempt for the gifts of God."[40] These examples give force to the author's warnings about the impossibility of restoration, and have clearly been chosen on account of the proximity to exclusion in which some among the community now find themselves: once they turn away from Christ and bring him dishonor, there is no repentance, no sacrifice, that can restore their standing in God's favor (6:6; 10:26).

The wilderness generation stands as an "example of disobedience" (4:11), into whose pattern some of the addressees are in danger of falling. The distrust (ἀπιστία) of the wilderness generation stands in stark contrast to the trust (πίστις) exemplified by the people of faith in Hebrews 11. We have seen how faith in chapter 11 is defined specifically within the context of patron-client relationships. Faith looks to God as Benefactor with unwavering trust, and, further, faith perseveres in that commitment to the Patron and in the course which leads to the reception of the benefaction.[41] In the example of the wilderness generation, one finds a picture of a group brought to the very border of their promised inheritance, who at the last panic in the face of their estimation of the native inhabitants, and withdraw their trust ("faith") from the God who promised them victory and a lasting inheritance. The author uses this paradigm to explicate the danger faced by the addressees. Having endured a period of wandering, as it were, in which they experienced the world's rejection and still held onto God's promise (10:32–34), some of the believers are wavering in their commitment at the very time when they are closer than ever to attaining what was promised. Some stand in danger of falling into distrust, of disobeying God by not continuing to assemble together to worship (10:25) and by dissociating from those in need (13:3), of regarding more the opinion and hostility of society than of the God who promises them an unshakable kingdom.

Warnings against Dishonoring the Divine Patron and Broker

Perceiving that the Christian community stands on the verge of dishonoring God in a manner similar to the wilderness generation and Esau, the author makes the addressees aware of the danger through a number of stern warnings designed to arouse fear and dread in the hearers of the consequences of pursuing a course which would provoke their Patron. These warnings appeal to the emotions of the hearers, and are thus an important part of the argument from *pathos*, an essential component of persuasion for the classical rhetorical theorists. The admonitions which are most crucial to this study appear in 6:4–8 and 10:26–31, for these explicitly draw on topics of patronage and the proper return for benefactions. The warnings appearing in 2:1–4; 3:12; 4:1; 10:35–38; and 12:15, while of secondary importance, also reflect the author's interest in drawing the addressees' attention to the honor of Christ and the favor of God, both of which stand to be violated should the community show a lack of πίστις.

Following the initial presentation of Jesus and declaration of his dignity as the Son, in whom God now speaks, the author offers this exhortation (2:1–4; RSV): "Therefore we must pay the closer attention to what we have heard, lest we drift away from it. For if the message declared by angels was valid and every transgression or disobedience received a just retribution, how shall we escape if we neglect such a great salvation?" The introduction of this passage with the logical connector Διὰ τοῦτο commands attention. It suggests that this warning against "drifting away" from the message, and so "neglecting so great a salvation," is the goal of the preceding section. In 1:5–14, the author demonstrated at length that the dignity of the Son surpassed that of the angels. In this warning, he first notes that every act of willful neglect against the message delivered by angels (i.e., the Torah) received the punishment which justice demanded. That is, the honor of the angels could only be restored—and it was necessary that it should be restored—by means of the punishment of those who had shown them contempt. A greater punishment, however, must await those who "neglect so great a salvation" as was gained by the Son for his clients at such cost to himself. Developing the honor of Christ in 1:1–14, therefore, enhances the severity of the insult offered to Christ where his message and gift are neglected. Inherent in the participle ἀμελήσαντες is the notion of showing contempt for the thing "neglected."[42] To show such neglect towards the promise of the gospel, and hence to affront the bearer of that message, would put one in greater danger than those who transgressed the Torah.

The second warning is built around the example of the wilderness generation, which in Psalm 95 is held up as a negative paradigm to each successive generation of worshippers. The danger facing the community is the possibility of apostasy, a choice which would follow from a faltering trust: "Take care, brethren, lest there be in any of you an evil, unbelieving heart (καρδία πονηρὰ ἀπιστίας), leading you to fall away (ἀποστῆναι) from the living God" (3:12; RSV). According to Danker, this καρδία πονηρὰ is a "base heart," which is "the root of a wicked life." Such a heart is neither capable of virtue "nor of recognizing it in others."[43] Hence the person having such a heart would not recognize the trustworthiness of the God who gives such great promises in Christ, and, distrusting God, would outrage the Deity. The author intimates that some of the addressees may be in danger of "turning from the living God." This phrase contains allusions to Jewish and Christian missionary language, particularly with regard to the implicit distinction between the one, true and "living" God and the many false, lifeless idols.[44] Since a great obstacle to the addressees' regaining their standing in society is their avoidance of all idolatrous activities, the author may be afraid that some of the members, desiring to reduce tension between them and the unbelieving society, are considering a return to engagement in the worship of idols which formed a prominent part of most every civic, social, economic, and political activity.

In light of the fate of the wilderness generation, who acted out their disregard for God through distrust and disobedience, the author, in an explicit appeal to their emotions, calls the addressees to be afraid (4:1): "Therefore, while the promise of entering his rest remains, let us fear lest any of you be judged to have fallen short." What causes fear is the presence of a highly valued good, referred to by the catchword "rest," from which a person may be excluded because of a lack of trust (4:2–3). The author hopes that by inciting a deep dread of provoking the Benefactor through distrust, the wavering among the addressees will be motivated to confirm their endurance in hope and trust in God.

Perhaps one of the most troublesome passages in the history of theological interpretation appears in 6:4–8, which constitutes a third section of strong admonition:

> For it is impossible to restore again to repentance those who have once been enlightened, who have tasted the heavenly gift, and have become partakers of the Holy Spirit, and have tasted the goodness of the word of God and the powers of the age to come, if they then commit apostasy, since they crucify the Son of God on their own account and hold him up to contempt. For land which has drunk the rain that often falls upon it, and brings forth vegetation useful to those for whose sake it is cultivated, receives a blessing from God. But if it bears thorns and thistles, it is worthless and near to being cursed; its end is to be burned (RSV).

While the author quickly encourages his audience after delivering these dire warnings that such could never be their fate, his words cannot have failed to have their impact (as they have had upon generations of readers). Indeed, by again arousing fear of the dread consequences of falling away, he helps assure that the faltering among the congregation will find the resources to persevere.

The author claims, however, no more than what was required by the Greco-Roman ethos, as expressed, for example, in Dio *Or.* 31.65: "those who insult their benefactors will by nobody be esteemed to deserve a favour." 6:4–6 contrasts the benefits which have been enjoyed by the believer (6:4–5), and which are full of promise for the future perfection of the gifts, with the strikingly inappropriate response of "turning away" from the one who has gained these gifts for the believer and "holding [him] up to public scorn." The one who "shrinks back unto destruction" (10:39), in refusing to endure what is required to keep these benefits, has esteemed them too lightly. The agricultural maxim which follows this warning is actually quite apt. Rain is regarded as a benefaction of God (cf. Matt 5:45b), which here looks for a proper return. God's gifts are to bring forth gratitude and loyalty toward God as well as useful fruits for the fellow-believers (cf. 6:10). Such a response will lead to the consummation of blessing. The improper response of breaking with the benefactor, indeed, bringing dishonor to the name of the benefactor, leads to the curse and the fire, that is, exclusion from the promise and exposure to the anger of the Judge.

The admonition of 10:26–31 presents the same severe result in even more heightened tone, seeking to augment the hearers' fear:

> For if we sin deliberately after receiving the knowledge of the truth, there no longer remains a sacrifice for sins, but a fearful prospect of judgment, and a fury of fire which will consume the adversaries. A man who has violated the law of Moses dies without mercy at the testimony of two or three witnesses. How much worse punishment do you think will be deserved by the man who has spurned the Son of God, and profaned the blood of the covenant by which he was sanctified, and outraged the Spirit of grace? For we know him who said, "Vengeance is mine, I will

repay." And again, "The Lord will judge his people." It is a
fearful thing to fall into the hands of the living God (RSV).

The passage sets up another "lesser to greater" argument
between infractions of the Mosaic covenant and transgression of the new covenant—the "willful sin" of 10:26, a
deliberate violation of the loyalty due the Patron who has
struck up a better alliance with the people. Just as the dignity of Christ exceeds that of Moses (cf. 3:1–6), so violations
of that dignity will incur a greater punishment than even
the "death without mercy" which fell upon those who disre-
garded Torah. This willful sin, a challenge to the honor of
Christ, will lead to τιμωρία, which Aulus Gellius (*Attic
Nights* 7.14.2–4) specifically links to the preservation of
"the dignity and prestige of the one who is sinned against
. . . lest the omission of punishment bring him into contempt and diminish the esteem in which he is held."

The one who assaults the honor of Christ, who should
rather enhance the honor of the patron, becomes the tar-
get for divine satisfaction, the restoration of the honor of
the Son. The one who fails to persevere in loyalty and obedience to Jesus manifests disregard for the gifts of God
and for the patron-client relationship with God through
Jesus. Thus the one who continues in sin (i.e., abandons
the people of God, cf. 11:25–26) "has regarded as profane
the blood of the covenant with which he or she was sanctified," the blood by which he or she has been given access
to God as Patron. The one who falters in trust and perseverance "has outraged the Spirit of grace (τὸ πνεῦμα τῆς
χάριτος ἐνυβρίσας)." Spicq comments that "one could
not make a more striking contrast than between ὕβρις
and χάρις,"[45] and indeed meeting favor and the promise
of benefaction with insult is at once highly inappropriate
and foolish. Dio (*Or.* 31.14) expresses the society's condemnation of such a return, going so far as to call it "impi-
ety" (ἀσέβεια). Those who turn thus from God's
beneficence in Christ encounter God no longer as

favorable Patron, but as Judge and Avenger (10:31). The threefold challenge to God invites God's response as Vindicator of the honor of the Son and the worth of the gifts which have been scorned. The explicit appeal to *pathos*, specifically "fear," resurfaces in 10:27, 31: nothing remains for the apostate but "a fearful (φοβερὰ) prospect of judgment" (10:27), who will learn what a "fearful thing (φοβερὸν)" it is "to fall into the hands of the living God" (10:31). Fear is again heightened by the declaration of the impossibility of restoration (10:26), for after rejecting the brokerage of Jesus there remains no mediator who can regain God's favor for the transgressor.[46]

Having aroused such fear in his audience, he has prepared and motivated them to consider how to avoid the course of action which would offer such an affront to God and turn beneficence into anger. It is at this point that he reminds them of their former display of loyalty to Christ and to one another (10:32–34), and the trust and hope they showed as their status and property in the world were stripped from them. Such a stance manifested the "confidence" (παρρησία), the opposite of fear, which springs from commitment to the benefactor and to attaining the reward God promised. The admonition of 10:35 urges the addressees to hold onto precisely this stance as the means to retain the favor of the benefactor. Throwing away their παρρησία and the reward which attaches to it would be to refuse the gifts of the benefactor, and hence to "do him despite." "Shrinking back" recalls the sin of the wilderness generation, who displayed their distrust of God and their disobedience by not pressing on in the journey to which God called them, but rather by seeking to turn back at the very threshold of the consummation of their hope and God's beneficence. For the addressees to shrink back now, that is, to seek to reacquire their place in the worldly homeland and ease the tension between their unbelieving neighbors and themselves, would mean that they would have "come short" of entering the promised rest (4:1)

and, indeed, fallen short of what God's beneficence promised. This is poignantly phrased in 12:15: "see to it that no
one falls short of God's favor." For those who have already
experienced God's benefaction, "who have tasted the
heavenly gift" (6:4–5), to fall short of God's favor is to fall
into God's anger.

Conclusions

The author's attitudes concerning apostasy are firmly
rooted in the socio-cultural values and expectations of the
Mediterranean. When one is taken into a patron-client
relationship, one inherits a set of obligations which the
virtuous person will dutifully perform. Accepting a benefit obligates one to show loyalty to the giver.[47] To violate
these obligations by returning insult and ingratitude to
one's benefactor was to vitiate a sacred bond which could
not be restored. Such a spurning of the debt one owed
one's patron, which amounted to contempt both for the
gifts and the giver, constituted a grave affront to the
honor of the benefactor and called for satisfaction. To
ignore or pass over such a violation of a privileged, intimate bond would not be an act of favor or "grace," but a
violation of one's own honor and worth. In the case of the
Christian abandoning his or her commitment to Jesus,
the stakes are higher than in any other patron-client
bond. Apostasy—whether the public denial or quiet drifting away—offers a grave affront to the only means of
access (i.e., broker) to God as patron and benefactor, thus
causing the offender to fall back into an adversarial relationship with God, the natural state before Jesus' mediation. The author calls for nothing more from the
addressees than that they live out in their relationship
with God and Christ the most basic virtues of the
Greco-Roman society, namely the demonstration of
proper honor and gratitude. This agenda unites the
didactic and hortatory sections of the letter, and so proves

to be an important key to understanding the argument
and purpose of the whole.

5
The Path to Honor

Honor and shame provide a group the means to enforce within that group conformity to the values and behaviors promoted by the group.[1] Within a complex society, however, there are many different groups using the same terms of value ("honor" and "dishonor") to motivate adherence to each particular group's traditions, commitments, and ideals. There are, therefore, as many "courts of reputation" as there are subgroups within a society. In chapter 3, we explored Hebrews' attempts to detach its recipients from concern for the opinion of non-Christian groups: the believers are to "despise shame," or consider as nothing the lack of esteem they have in society's eyes, in order to be free to pursue Christian values, ideals, and commitments. This is the "deconstructionist" aspect of the strategy of most minority cultures in the ancient Mediterranean. The positive counterpart is the establishment of an alternate court of opinion—the designation of a body of "significant others" before whom one is to feel "shame," and whose approval and esteem one is to seek. This alternate court of opinion is generally limited to the members of the group, so that concern for honor and esteem leads to the fulfillment of the group's program. As a sort of compensator for the awareness that the group represents a minority opinion, the court of reputation is extended to include some super-social force (e.g., God, Nature, or Truth) which also bears witness to the honor of the group member. The opinion and evaluation of the majority, of course, is unreliable precisely because the majority is not devoted to this higher Judge and the standards of that court.[2]

Thus the author of Hebrews frequently turns the addressees' attention to the alternate court of reputation, the body of those significant others whose opinion and approval one ought to seek through perseverance in the group's values and ideals. Within Hebrews, as in most early Christian literature, this "court" is formed by God and Christ as the judges whose verdicts have eternal validity, and by the visible community, which reinforces the worth and honor of its members according to the standards projected onto the heavenly court. While the author urges the addressees to be unmindful of the esteem or lack of esteem in society's eyes, he also seeks to spur on their desire for honor in the eyes of the group and in God's sight.

The Alternate Court of Reputation

The Jewish and Christian conviction that God was the final Judge of all human affairs proved to be a powerful instrument in refocusing the individual's desire for approval and honor. The conviction that, in God's sight, one's behavior was honorable could be enough to offset the disapproval and rejection of society. This was certainly the case for Paul, who frequently contrasts the approval of human beings and the approval of God, claiming that he sought only the latter without regard for the former (1 Thess 2:4; Gal 1:10; cf. Rom 2:29).[3] For both Paul and the author of Hebrews, God's vindication of Jesus manifests both the radical difference between God's evaluation and the world's and the ability of God's verdict to overturn the verdict of the lower court. Where the unbelieving society condemned Jesus to the most severe humiliation (12:2), God has granted him the place of greatest honor. Because God has the last word on a person's honor, the divine court of opinion is elevated above any human court which opposes God's standards and criteria of evaluation.

The author frequently calls the audience to attend to God's evaluation, warning and encouraging them to show the greatest concern for God's opinion. The passage which is so frequently used to preach about the power of Scripture, namely 4:12–13, actually pertains more to God as Judge of the totality of human life:

> For the word of God is living and active, sharper than any two-edged sword, piercing to the division of soul and spirit, of joints and marrow, and discerning the thoughts and intentions of the heart. And before him no creature is hidden, but all are open and laid bare to the eyes of him with whom we have to do (RSV).

It is thus an admonition to the addressees to have a care that the whole of their lives be carried on with a view to God's approval, for indeed all of life is subject to God's inquiry and will be evaluated not by the standards approved by society, but by God.[4] The author also closes his oration by pointing the addressees to the approval of God: "Now may the God of peace . . . equip you with everything good that you may do his will, working in you that which is pleasing in his sight, through Jesus Christ" (13:20–21; RSV). The goal of the believer's life, therefore, is to please God, that is, to live by God's standards of honorable behavior and so gain God's approval and testimony, which count above all others' esteem.[5]

The inhabitants of the ancient world relied on an honorable remembrance to keep their honor alive after their deaths. The society's recollection of one's noble deeds, benefactions, and the like assured the blessing of one's name living on in honor. For the author of Hebrews, God's memory preserves the individual's honor. He assures the addressees that God remembers their acts of love and service, which assures them of approval and future reward (6:10; RSV): "For God is not so unjust as to forget your work and the love which you showed for his sake in serving the saints, as you still do." In the same way, the fact that sins are removed from God's memory assures the believers that their honor in God's sight will be untarnished and undiminished (10:17). The believer may stand before God's court of reputation with confidence, knowing that God's recollection of his or her noble deeds (as defined by the Christian minority culture) will guarantee eternal honor: the disgrace which the "deviant" and marginalized community attains in the society's memory counts for nothing, since God's court will overturn their verdict.

The strongest expression of God as the most "significant other" appears in the references to the last judgement, when the divine evaluation of all people will be made manifest. In light of the coming "Day," that is, the day of judgement, the author urges his hearers to encourage one another in doing the noble deeds which will result in honor before that court: "Let us consider how to stir up one another to love and good works, not neglecting to meet together, as is the habit of some, but encouraging one another, and all the more as you see the Day drawing near" (10:24–25; RSV). On that day, the visible realm will be removed and the invisible world disclosed (12:26–27): thus the people of faith who have evaluated and acted with the invisible world in view (11:3, 7, 27) will be vindicated. Those who have remained loyal (πιστός) to their Patron will receive the promised reward and salvation (9:28), while those who have enacted ingratitude through apostasy, or have otherwise transgressed God's values, will receive lasting disgrace (cf. 10:29–31). Fear of God's censure is made to outweigh fear of society's censure, in order to preserve the group's values.[6]

Moxnes's comment about Paul is equally true for Hebrews: "It is before God's court that the final decision on honour or shame is made. Thus, the ultimate 'significant other' is God."[7] The author shares Paul's convictions that evaluations derived from the visible realm are unreliable, being based on the temporary, visible realm (cf. 2 Cor 4:16–18). True and reliable evaluations must be based on the eternal, invisible realities. The person who seeks lasting honor, therefore, must look not to the approval of those who evaluate by the standards of this shadowy reality, but rather to the opinion of the One who evaluates from the perspective of the eternal realities.[8] Just as Jesus cared only for God's approval and the honor which God would confer, so the addressees are urged to value God's approval above all else. This would lead them to continue in obedience to God's standards, that is, to value themselves according to the standards of the Christian culture.

For the author of Hebrews, the community of believers forms the visible body of significant others which reinforces the divine criteria for evaluation, that is, the ideals and values of the Christian culture. The community praises and censures its members, and as long as the interaction between members remains frequent and vibrant, its members will seek approval primarily in the community's estimation. Members will thus seek honor and self-worth in terms of the alternative court's definitions of honorable and praiseworthy behavior. Part of the hortatory purpose of Hebrews concerns the maintenance of this alternate court. The author expresses concern for the waning commitment of some, who are "neglecting to meet together" (10:25). A strong group commitment and a high level of group interaction and reinforcement of group values are essential for keeping members from looking again to the unbelieving society for the affirmation of their self-worth, and thence to returning to the behaviors and ideals valued by the dominant Greco-Roman culture.

The final parenesis (10:19–13:24) contains several exhortations aimed specifically at reinforcing the vitality of the community as the body of significant others for each member. First, the author calls the audience to "draw near" to God through the way opened up in Christ. This is, however, none other than a call to gather for the worship of the common assembly, a fact made explicit in 10:24–25: "Let us consider how to stir up one another to love and good works, not neglecting to meet together, as is the habit of some, but encouraging one another, and all the more as you see the Day drawing near." The author thus directs the community to remind one another of what constitutes valued and praiseworthy behavior, and to spur one another on to act nobly in the eyes of the group. The author seeks to strengthen the social base of support for Christian activity and commitment—the "plausibility structure," which makes it possible for individuals to hold onto their view of reality in an atmosphere of competing definitions of reality (e.g., Christian vs. Jewish or Greco-Roman views).[9] Within the community, members are to assure one another of their honor and worth on the basis of the criteria of the gospel (as opposed to the criteria of the outside world, cf. Jas 2:1–7; 1 Cor 11:22), and thus offset the negative messages the members are getting about their behavior from the larger society.

Throughout the letter, the author directs the addressees to reinforce the commitment of each of its members, and particularly to look out for those who are in danger of abandoning the community in favor of the esteem of outsiders:

> Watch out, brothers and sisters, lest there be in any of you an evil, unbelieving heart, leading you to fall away from the living God. But exhort one another every day, as long as it is called "today," that none of you may be hardened by the deceitfulness of sin (3:12–13; author's trans. cf. 4:1; 12:15–16).

The community is given collective responsibility for reinforcing the loyalty and commitment of each member, to praise those who enact the group's values, and to assure the wavering. If the addressees take up the watchful stance urged by the author, it should be impossible for any individual to doubt that here, in the circle of believers, are his or her significant others, whose opinion alone counts. The author himself acts as part of this alternate court of opinion, censuring the addressees for their waning fervor and lack of zeal (5:11–14), praising them for their displays of love service (6:9–10) and for their former demonstration of commitment even at great cost (10:32–34). The community leaders will also function as an important part of this alternate court, ascribing honor to the obedient and committed, rebuking the half-hearted (13:17).

The apparently unrelated exhortations of chapter 13 in fact continue the author's interests in maintaining a strong group culture. He urges that "familial love" (φιλαδελφία, 13:1) continue, so that members of the community will continue to regard fellow-believers as kin, and so as the primary source of one's identity and honor, as well as the primary group to whom one owes one's first duty and allegiance. The exhortation to provide hospitality for travelling fellow-believers (13:2) links the local Christian community to the broader Christian minority culture. The author urges solidarity with those whom society has targeted as deviants (13:3; cf. 10:32–34; 11:25): only the group that is willing to support its members under such conditions can maintain the loyalty and trust of its adherents, and show that society's court is not, after all, the final adjudicator of worth.

The alternate court of reputation is further broadened to include the historic community of faith—namely the "encircling cloud of witnesses" (12:1) of the past exemplars of faith, who now watch and judge the addressees' performance in their "contest."[10] While the visible community may be small, and its evaluation of the individual perhaps insignificant when compared to the esteem of the dominant majority, the invisible community which evaluates and ascribes honor by the same standards is overwhelming, spanning generations and transcending the earthly realm:

> You have come to Mount Zion and to the city of the living God, the heavenly Jerusalem, and to innumerable angels in festal gathering, and to the assembly of the first-born who are enrolled in heaven, and to a judge who is God of all, and to the spirits of just men made perfect, and to Jesus, the mediator of a new covenant, and to the sprinkled blood that speaks more graciously than the blood of Abel (12:22–24; RSV).

Before *this* expansive court the believer is called to seek everlasting prestige. While the author seeks to neutralize any sense of shame the addressees may have in the sight of unbelievers—that is, urge them to regard as nothing the evaluation of outsiders, and hence to live free of the pressures to conform to the norms of non-Christians—he also seeks to strengthen their sense of shame before one another (before the alternate "court of reputation"), so that their desire for honor may be fulfilled specifically through their Christian witness and commitments.

The Foundations of Christian Honor

Minority cultures will often ground the honor of their members on a significantly different basis from the criteria used in the dominant culture.[11] For the author of Hebrews, the believer's honor is grounded in his or her relationship to Christ. Through association with Jesus, the most honored figure in the Jewish-Christian cosmos (cf. 1:1–13; 2:6–9; 3:1–6; 10:12–13), the believer receives his or her strongest claim to honor and worth. A primary rhetorical purpose for the development of Jesus' honor is to establish the honor of the "many sons and daughters" of 2:10,[12] who must wait the final inheritance of their adoptive birthright. Ultimately, the believers' adoption as children of God provides them with a peerless dignity and a ground for self-respect (cf. Sir 3:11, which links a person's honor with that of his or her father).[13]

The connection between Christ and his followers is expressed in the language of kinship, as in 2:11–12. They enjoy a common origin (God), and so share in the collective honor of God's house. Christ's rise to a seat at God's right hand promises honor for all believers, since "the advance of one member of an agnatic family would advantage all his kindred."[14] The believers are members of a household of which God is the head and over which Christ rules as Son and heir (3:6; 10:21), and as such share in the honor of the head of the house, and come under his patronage and protection. Adoption into God's family brings the believers into the sacred lineage of Abraham (2:17), an "ideological genealogy"[15] which gives the believers an enhanced sense of self-worth as members of God's chosen and redeemed community. The connection between Christ and Christians is further emphasized where the author uses the language of friendship or partnership ("partners of Christ," 3:14; "partners in a heavenly calling," 3:1). The believer is assured a share in the honor and dignity which Jesus has attained (cf. Matt 19:28; John 17:22), an inheritance they too will enjoy as children of God (1:14; 6:17; 9:15; 12:28).

The believers' dignity is also established through the author's claims for their holiness or purity in God's sight. The language of purification, sanctification, and forgiveness of sins, which occupies the central portion of Hebrews (7:11–10:18) assures the addressees that the obstacles to honor before God have been decisively removed in Christ. As long as they remain faithful and obedient, they need not fear divine punishment for their sins (which are, essentially, affronts to God's honor; cf. 10:29). The believers are "holy" (3:1), set apart to stand in the presence of God as Patron. With their purification (1:3; 2:17; 9:12, 14; 10:22) came the wiping away of all marks against their honor before God's court, such that they now stand with confidence before God, and are able to receive the full dignity of adoption by God.

The believers' direct access to God, attained for them by Jesus, is itself a great privilege and token of honor. In Israel, access to God was attainable only in proportion to one's dignity or standing within the Jewish people: Gentiles had distant access; then the Israelite women, the common Israelite men, the Levites, and the priests enjoyed increasing access to the throne of God in the Holy of Holies, each group being able to approach one step closer, as it were. Only the high priest could enter God's presence in the Holy of Holies.[16] Hebrews confers the exceptional dignity of the high priest, in effect, on the believing community, since they now enjoy full access to the throne of grace (4:16; cf. 10:19–20). Indeed, the quality of this access exceeds that to which even the priests are entitle: "We have an altar from which those who serve the tabernacle have no right to eat" (13:10). Implicit in this is a claim for the greater honor of the believers on the basis of this greater privilege.

Finally, the believers' honor rests upon God's confession of association with them, by which God imparts to them a share in the divine honor and commits to preserve their honor as an extension of God's own dignity. As the "people of God" (4:9), that is, the "people called by God's name," the Christians' honor is guaranteed by God.[17] Just as God owned the exemplars of faith who rejected inclusion in any earthly homeland in favor of persevering in the quest for a home with God (11:16), so God will give testimony for all who confess that they are "sojourners and foreigners on the earth," thus bearing witness to God.[18]

The author of Hebrews thus demonstrates to his audience that the true basis for their honor is to be found in the benefits achieved for them by Christ—adoption into God's family and access to God's "throne of favor." While breaking off the association would constitute an affront to God and Christ, and so incur God's wrath and vengeance for God's injured dignity, such a break would also separate the believers from their own claim to honor.

Both aspects contribute to the power of the author's
appeal for perseverance in faith and obedience.

The Reinterpretation of Disgrace

From within the framework of the Christian counterculture, the author is able to reinterpret the believers' experience of disgrace at the hands of the dominant culture.
By attaching positive significance to these experiences
from within the alternative culture, the author hopes not
only to undermine the force of society's attempts at social
control (i.e., by shaming the "deviants' back into conformity with the norms of the dominant culture), but even
make these same experiences an occasion for strengthening commitment to the minority culture by turning the
experiences of disgrace into tokens of honor and promises of greater reward.

First, the author recasts the believers' experiences of
ridicule, trial, loss of status and property, and endurance
of continued reproach as the training or discipline by God
of God's adopted children. The community's endurance
of society's rejection and censure, in fact turns out to be
the token of God's acceptance and discipline (12:5–11),
whereby the addressees are fitted to receive their birthright and to enjoy the honor toward which God leads
them (2:10):

> Have you forgotten the exhortation which addresses
> you as sons?— "My son, do not regard lightly the disci-
> pline of the Lord, nor lose courage when you are punished
> by him. For the Lord disciplines him whom he loves, and
> chastises every son whom he receives." It is for discipline
> that you have to endure. God is treating you as sons; for
> what son is there whom his father does not discipline? If
> you are left without discipline, in which all have partici-
> pated, then you are illegitimate children and not sons.
> Besides this, we have had earthly fathers to discipline us
> and we respected them. Shall we not much more be subject
> to the Father of spirits and live? (12:5–9; RSV)

The believers' struggle to hold onto their confession in the face of society's hostility and censure is their endurance in παιδεία, the "education" by which all parents mold the character of their children.[19] What society intends, therefore, as an experience of disgrace aimed at bringing the deviant back into line with the values of the dominant culture becomes the proof of the believers' adoption into God's family and a powerful encouragement to persevere in their commitments to the minority group. Only those who have shared in discipline (12:8) will also share the rewards as "partners of Christ" (3:14) and "partners in a heavenly calling" (3:1).[20] The believers may even cherish their marginalization and censure by society as a process by which their character is tried and proven, and which guarantees their future honor and vindication.[21]

Second, the author uses the image of the contest (ἀγών) to speak of the traumatic experience of public disgrace and social and economic disenfranchisement suffered by the believers (10:32–44). The author sums up this experience as an ἄθλησις, "competition," the rhetorical force of which was well recognized by Chrysostom, himself a part of the ancient Mediterranean honor culture: "Moreover he did not say 'trials' (πειρασμοὺς) but 'contest' (ἄθλησιν), which is an expression of commendation and of very great praise."[22] A more extended use of this imagery appears in the exhortation built around the example of Jesus in 12:1–4:

> Therefore, since we have so great an encircling cloud of witnesses, let us also lay aside every weight, and the sin which clings so closely, and let us run with perseverance the race (ἀγῶνα) that is set before us, looking to Jesus the pioneer and perfecter of our faith, who for the joy that was set before him endured the cross, despising the shame, and is seated at the right hand of the throne of God. Consider him who endured from sinners such hostility against himself, so that you may not grow weary or fainthearted. In

your struggle against sin you have not yet resisted to the
point of shedding your blood (RSV, modified).

The heroes of faith are not only "witnesses" to God and
the promised reward: the image of the "encircling cloud of
witnesses" conjures up the image of the spectators of competitions or games, from whom the competitors seek
honor and esteem. Like those who compete in races, the
believers are to "lay aside" every thing which might impede
their running: they are to set aside "sin" as if it were a cling-
ing garment which restricted their movement toward the
prize.[23] They compete against sin, their antagonist (πρὸς
τὴν ἁμαρτίαν ἀνταγωνιζόμενοι, 12:4) in this contest
(ἀγών, 12:1). Finally, as runners clear their minds of all
distractions and set their eyes wholly toward the goal, so
the believers are to fix their gaze on Jesus, who have run
ahead to the victory in which all may share (12:2).

In an honor culture like the Greco-Roman world, athletic competitions held a great appeal, affording the victors in the various events an opportunity for achieving
fame. It quickly became a realm of metaphors by which
spokespersons of minority cultures could set the disgrace
and abuse suffered by their adherents (which parallel the
rigors of athletic training) in the light of an honorable
competition for victory.[24] Philosophers such as Epictetus
make extensive use of athletic imagery, recasting the
struggle against difficulties or the reproach of society as a
wrestling match in which the philosopher who endures is
promised an honorable victory (cf. *Diss.* 1.24.1–2;
1.18.21). Both Epictetus and Dio Chrysostom speak of the
life of the Cynic philosopher as an athletic contest.
Although the Cynic deliberately seeks to place himself
outside of society's evaluation, seeking the margins and
extremes of human existence, his life is still an "Olympic
contest" (Epictetus, *Diss.* 3.22.52). The hardships he
suffers, such as sleeping out of doors, going hungry, and
other straits which are interpreted by members of the

dominant culture as a depraved and disgraceful existence, are interpreted from within the minority culture as
divine training by Zeus (*Diss*. 3.22.56) and as participation
in a noble competition for virtue (cf. Dio, *Or*. 8.11–13).

One finds similar uses of athletic imagery in the literature of the Jewish minority culture, again as an image by
which to turn the status-degrading experiences of the
faithful Jews into a quest for honor before God. 4
Maccabees speaks of a series of executions, which would
have been regarded as the shameful death of deviants by
the members of the dominant culture, as just such a
quest.[25] The brothers are praised as athletes (ἀσκήτας)
and competitors (ἀγωνισταί, 12:15), their tortures
becomes a contest (ἀγών), the Gentile king's court an
"arena" (γυμνασία, 11:20). The disgrace of punishment
and mutilation becomes a "noble contest" (16:16). Near
the conclusion, the author summarizes the whole action
of the narrative sections of his oration within an extended
athletic metaphor comparable in scope to Heb 12:1–4: In
the divine contest (ἀγὼν θεῖος), Eleazar was the first con-
testant (προηγωνίζετο), the mother of the seven
brother competed (ἐνήθλει), the seven brothers partici-
pated in the contest (ἠγωνίζετο), and Antiochus IV was
the antagonist (ἀντηγωνίζετο). The victors received the
wreath from Piety herself (4 Macc 17:11–16).

The author of Hebrews thus applies a firmly established tradition to the needs of his audience. Moreover,
interpreting the addressees' experience as a contest
allows the author to harness the widely praised virtue of
Courage, and to define it as perseverance or "endurance"
in Christian community and activity. Endurance is both a
prominent aspect of Courage (cf. *Rhet. ad Her*. 3.2.3:
"courage is . . . the endurance of hardship in expectation
of profit") and a prominent feature of the author's exhortation. As Jesus endured both cross and contradiction
(12:2–3), so the addressees are called to endure in their
contest (12:1) and in God's training (12:7). Faith as a

demonstration of courage, channeled toward maintaining their Christian commitment, ennobles their experience of dishonor and rejection at society's hands.

The third way by which the author transforms the believers' experience of disgrace is through the examples of Christ, Abraham, Moses, and the martyrs (see chapter 3). The author creates a pattern by which persevering in the face of reproach and abuse leads to esteem and joy before the court of God: the blessedness of the end ennobles the means to that end. Since the shame of the cross led to Christ's exaltation, the believers have the assurance that their own "contest" will result in honor before God.[26]

The community's experience of disgrace and rejection at the hands of the unbelieving society, far from being a sign of their lack of honor and their deviance, becomes a source of assurance for their worth and future reward. Their perseverance in the face of society's means of social control (e.g., dishonor and rejection) is in fact a noble contest in which the believers compete for a heavenly prize, and a sign of their adoption by God and the training by which they are fitted to be God's children. It is the path to honor pursued by Abraham, Moses, the martyrs, and Jesus himself—those who walk such a path need fear no disgrace, for their honor is assured by God and God's Son.

The Path to Honor

We have seen how the author of Hebrews appeals to the emotions of the hearers as part of his overall strategy of persuasion—particularly prominent have been fear, confidence, and emulation. Fear is attached to the course of action which would affront God or Christ, and hence result in punishment and disgrace before the divine court of reputation (10:26–31; see chapter 4). Within the alternate court which the author has constructed, the only threat to the believers' honor comes form their own wavering or falling away. Apostasy is the gravest danger to the believer's honor, as a violation of God's favor and beneficence. Such a failure to return the obedience and loyalty which a client owes a patron not only invites retribution, but also shows the client to be shameless and untrustworthy, hence dishonorable.[27] What the addressees are to fear is the possibility of failing to attain the prize for which they entered the contest, falling short of the honor and reward which God has held out before them (cf. 4:1; 12:15). Hence, the threat to honor is not external but internal, where the believer's commitment and boldness waver.

Those who remain committed, however, may enjoy the confidence which comes from having the help and resources of God ready at hand, and stand assured of the reward which God has prepared. Here the author may stir up the addressees' ambition, speaking of the greatness of the prize for which they contend and the immeasurable dignity promised to them as children of God. At the same time, the author channels their ambition wholly toward the fulfillment of the minority culture's values and ideals, so that they are not drawn back again into concern for the honors which the unbelieving society offers.

One term by which the author appeals to his hearers' ambition is "inheritance"—the root κληρονομ- appears eleven times in Hebrews, a disproportionate number when compared to its occurrence in other New Testament documents. Pursuing an inheritance affords honor in two stages: the heir of a powerful figure, by virtue of standing to inherit, already enjoys considerable prestige and status (cf. Moses in 11:24); the heir also looks forward to greater honor still, when the inheritance is actually conferred. Those who are named heirs by God stand to gain inestimable honor, such that John Chrysostom can say with regard to Esau's poor trade (12:17) that he "lost the greatest honor and glory."[28] This inheritance is described in general terms as salvation (1:14; 5:9; 9:28) or "what was promised" (10:36; 6:12, 17; 9:15). The reader is assured, however, that it will be nothing short of the "glory" (δόξα, 2:10) enjoyed by the children of God. Even as Jesus awaits his full entrance into his inheritance ("the subjection of all things," 2:6–9; the "subjection" of his enemies "as a footstool under his feet," 1:13; 10:13), so the believers may gain the wherewithal to persevere through reflecting on their share in Christ's supreme dignity as his partners (3:14). The lack of honor the believers now suffer may be accepted and endured as prerequisite to the fulfillment of their ambition.[29] Their faith, or loyalty to God and trust in God's promises, is the assurance of their inheritance.[30]

The author spurs the believers on in endurance and commitment to the Christian life through assuring them of the greatness of the prize. The promised reward (10:35; 11:26; cf. 6:10) affords the believers all that they have lost in society, or cannot attain in the dominant culture, because of the group's values and ideals.[31] While they have suffered disenfranchisement from the society, they are promised citizenship in the city which God has founded (11:16; 13:14), a place in the heavenly homeland (11:16), indeed, an "unshakable kingdom" (12:28). While they have suffered the plundering of their property, they are promised "better and lasting possessions" (10:34). Although they have limited (if any) access to secular patrons, they enjoy access to the patronage of God, and look forward to a place within the heavenly sanctuary in the presence of God, where Jesus has entered as a forerunner on their behalf (6:19–20). The believers have already all but attained this reward (cf. 6:10; 10:35), and must now exercise their diligence to persevere and not fall short after they have come so far (4:11; 6:11). When the author includes the exhortation to be content with what they currently possess (13:5), he is not merely using a standard piece of moral instruction irrelevant to the addressees' situation:[32] given their loss of possessions (10:34), this is a pointed prohibition against seeking to regain goods and status in society at the cost of losing their reward. Their temperance now will permit them to attain the "better and lasting possessions" in the city of God.

What is the way by which the believers are to pursue and attain the reward and dignity to which God leads them? First, the believers are to maintain their identity as an alternative culture within the Greco-Roman society, and to continue to provide strong social support to the group's members. They must seek distinction in acts of love and service to fellow believers, which will lead them to attain their hope (6:10–11). They must persevere in their commitment to the group, resisting the attraction of sin, that is, of withdrawing from solidarity with the Christian community in favor of easing the tension in their relationship with the society (10:23–25; 13:3). This requirement is fortified by the author's crafting of the example of Moses and of the community's past victory in the contest (11:25–26//10:32–34). Achieving the promised reward, and the honor of citizenship in the heavenly city, requires loyalty to God's people (11:26//10:35). This solidarity reaches beyond the local community to the broader Christian minority culture, seen, for example, in the author's concern for hospitality.

The way to honor requires maintaining one's focus on God and God's reward, while remaining detached from the attraction of the world. The benefits of the worldly patrons will fail, for no earthly thing will survive the eschatological "shaking" (12:26–27): only the benefits given by the divine patron will endure into the eternal age. The believer must therefore hold onto the confidence, hope, and boast (or, claim to honor) given by God (3:6, 14; 10:23, 35), and "endure" for the sake of the better possessions, the better homeland, the better city (6:12; 10:36; 12:1, 7).[33] Faith is the central virtue for Hebrews, as faith enables endurance. People who have faith, that is, "trust" God to provide what God has promised, will receive an eternal grant of honor, God giving "attestation" or testimony (11:2) to the believer's dignity and worth. People who show faith, that is, remain loyal to Christ and the community, will enjoy the continued patronage of God—for these do not "shrink back," wavering in their loyalty and provoking their Benefactor (10:38–39). By faith, the believers will be able to choose the status of outsider and deviant now in order to attain the better citizenship of the city of God, lack of esteem and hardship now with God's people in order to receive the honor of all children of God when Christ returns.

The path to true and lasting honor involves embracing the experience of God's discipline (παιδεία, 12:5–9), which shapes the believer's character and refines his or her commitment. What society offers as dishonor, intending by slighting or reproach or rejection to force the believer back into line with society's values and goals, is actually the path to honor before God. As such, the honor-sensitive believer may overturn society's estimation of his or her convictions and decisions, knowing the end which God has appointed for the person of faith. The believer thus chooses to follow Jesus, "bearing his reproach" (13:13), leaving behind the concern for advancement as the unbelieving world defines it in favor of progress in virtue and nobility as God has revealed it. Within the fellowship of those who share a common hope, common values, and common commitment, the believer will enjoy adequate support and compensation for the disapproval of outsiders.

The way for the believer to preserve and augment honor is in the exercise of piety and gratitude (12:28; 13:15). The Christian must guide his or her actions so as to show care for the honor of Jesus, through whom he or she is adopted into God's family (12:5), enjoys access to God as Patron (4:16), and receives the promise of an eternal habitation (13:14). As an honorable client, the believer must show gratitude—not merely in feeling thankful, but in bearing testimony to the gracious favor of the Benefactor and in maintaining loyalty to God and

God's people without regard for one's own reputation and well-being (cf. Seneca, *Ep.* 81.27). The author invites the addressees to return praise and service to God and to his or her fellow believer (12:28; 13:15–16) as the proper response to God's gifts and promises. In the face of society's hostility and use of the negative sanction of dishonor, the believer's eternal honor is assured: those who persevere in faith will receive their inheritance at the time of God's visitation.

Conclusion

Attending to the language of honor and dishonor in the Letter to the Hebrews has brought us to a closer understanding of the situation of the addressees and the strategic response to that situation formulated by the author. People who have lost their esteem in society's estimation on account of their response to the gospel, beginning to feel again the longing for at-homeness in the world, are encouraged to set aside as nothing the negative feedback they receive from their former associates and unbelieving peers, and to persevere in their quest for greater and lasting honor in the kingdom of God. People who have begun to desire re-entry into the networks of patronage, and to reclaim their access to goods, services, and advancement, are directed to have a care for the honor of the Patron they have acquired in God at such great cost to Jesus, the broker and mediator of that relationship. The only fitting and rewarding channel for the satisfaction of their longing for esteem and self-worth is in mutual love and service in the believing community, and continued loyalty and gratitude toward their Benefactor.

As such, Hebrews is made to speak to our situation as followers of the Way. First, it cautions us to take God's honor seriously, and thus not to take sin lightly. It shows us that God's favor and wrath are not in fact two separate faces, a view shown in the frequent opposition of the God of the Old Testament and the God of Jesus by many theologians and lay persons throughout the centuries. God's anger and judgement are, rather, integral to one another:

precisely where God's favor, benefactions, and promises have been rejected in favor of the deceitful promises of the world and sin—where God's favor and gifts have been so lightly valued that one would choose the temporary pleasures of following the world's way over God's way—there favor is exchanged for wrath. The favor that was despised gives rise to anger and judgement. This does not limit God's freedom, or undermine God's mercy. Rather, it restores the immense value of God's gracious favor, so often taken for granted and held as a cheap and readily available commodity.

We have argued that the author's admonitions about the impossibility of restoring the apostate to repentance are part of an emotional appeal and therefore not the basis for a doctrine of "unpardonable sin." Nevertheless, one should leave the study of Hebrews with a greater awareness that the gifts God has provided—the salvation and inclusion into God's family which cost the Son his life—must be appropriately valued. This means that loyalty to God, the Giver, and to Christ, the Broker, must always be faithfully maintained and enacted in the ways God directs, such as in acts of love and service to other members of God's family and in bearing testimony to God's purposes, values, and gifts. When we slacken in our devotion to God and in the concrete expressions of that devotion out of a desire to gain patrons in the unbelieving world, or to advance in society's eyes, we risk affronting our Benefactor, and trading our eternal inheritance for "a single meal" (12:16).

Hebrews also shows us that we must be very intentional about establishing and preserving Christian community if we are to fulfill our calling to discipleship. People cannot help but be influenced in their thinking, evaluating, and decision-making by the opinions of others, and Western society has a way of bombarding its inhabitants with hundreds of messages daily about what it holds to be truly valuable, praiseworthy, and important.

Christians may still benefit from taking the exhortations of the author of Hebrews about strengthening their alternative culture to heart. Believers need to gather frequently with one another, both in the formal settings of worship and informally for support and encouragement in pursuing values that do not always reflect the values of our society. In their interactions with one another, believers are called to hold up as valuable for one another the ideals that God values and the actions which Jesus commands, discovering and discussing these together in study of the sacred texts, and encouraging one another to seek out ways of living them out. The voices of unbelievers are not likely to support such goals and actions, indeed often seem to push us in the opposite direction, trying to stir up greed, prejudice, or self-serving attitudes. Only with the strong support of others who are committed to the visions of humanity and community in the Scriptures can believers hope to remain on course toward their eternal homeland.

As we read about the honor culture which Hebrews addresses, we find that we, too, live in something of an honor culture. While the word "honor" is not frequently used in conversation, we are often drawn into evaluating others and ourselves by profession, salary, possessions, education, networks of influence ("the right crowd"), and the like. Hebrews reminds us that today, as then, society's criteria for evaluating a person's "success" or "worth" differ widely from Christ's criteria. When the author urges his audience to "despise shame," he speaks also to us, who must be willing to "make less of ourselves" in terms of the world's way of valuing in order to live out fully the truth of the gospel. If following Jesus means caring for the homeless or shut-ins rather than networking with the powerful and well-connected; if fulfilling the call to discipleship means freeing time to serve others or seek God's will rather than devote every possible hour to "getting ahead" at work or at school; if responding to God's love means buying less expensive clothes and cars in order to have more to give to others in need of even food and shelter: then we are to "despise shame," embrace being a little lower on society's ladder of status, or even off the ladder entirely, in order to be honorable persons in the sight of God. It is our confession that, ultimately, it is God's evaluation of our lives and labors that counts, and it is in light of that court of opinion that we are to weigh our decisions, desires, and dreams. It is also our confession that the reward of following God's way will more than compensate for what we "lose" in terms of the temporary and empty rewards of this world. Hebrews thus encourages us to follow boldly where Jesus leads, even where this brings us into criticism, reproach, even rejection by the unbelieving society. Knowing the love and beneficence of God, the reader is emboldened to embrace marginalization for the sake of Christ, to "bear his reproach," and continue in love, service, and in witness to the better hope which is found in God.

Notes

Chapter 1

1   Luke T. Johnson, *The Writings of the New Testament* (Philadelphia: Fortress, 1984), 412.

2   E.g., Ernst Käsemann, *The Wandering People of God* (Minneapolis: Augsburg, 1984 [1957]), and Gerd Theissen, *Untersuchungen zum Hebräerbrief* (Gütersloh: Gerd Mohn, 1969).

3   E.g., Ronald Williamson, *Philo and the Epistle to the Hebrews* (Leiden: E. J. Brill, 1970).

4   E.g., C. K. Barrett, "The Eschatology of the Epistle to the Hebrews," in *Background of the New Testament and Its Eschatology*, ed. by W. D. Davies and D. Daube (Cambridge: University Press, 1956).

5   Thompson, *The Beginnings of Christian Philosophy* (Washington, DC: The Catholic Biblical Association of America, 1982), 15.

6   A. W. Adkins, *Merit and Responsibility: A Study in Greek Values* (Oxford: University Press, 1960), 153–194.

7   Adkins, *Merit*, 185.

8   J. Pitt-Rivers, "Honour and Social Status," in J. G. Peristiany (ed.), *Honour and Shame: The Values of Mediterranean Society* (London: Weidenfeld and Nicolson, 1966).

9   Pitt-Rivers, "Honour," 21–25, 27, 35–36.

10   Pitt-Rivers, 22.

11   John H. Elliott, *A Home for the Homeless: A Social-Scientific Investigation of 1 Peter* (Minneapolis: Fortress, 1990), 8.

12   For a basic introduction to the methods and fruits of rhetorical criticism, the reader may refer to George A. Kennedy, *New Testament Interpretation through Rhetorical Criticism* (Chapel Hill, NC: University of North Carolina, 1984), and Burton L. Mack, *Rhetoric and the New Testament* (Minneapolis: Fortress, 1990). Some

landmark commentaries rooted firmly in rhetorical criticism include H. D. Betz, *Galatians* (Hermeneia; Philadelphia: Fortress, 1979), H. W. Attridge, *Hebrews* (Hermeneia; Philadelphia: Fortress, 1989), and Ben Witherington III, *Conflict and Community in Corinth* (Grand Rapids, MI: Eerdmans, 1995).

13 This is especially prominent in the opening sentence, in the Greek of course.

14 The use of "By faith" in chapter 11 offers an extensive example of this.

15 A similar hortatory peroration appears in Dio's eulogy for the boxer, Melancomas (*Or.* 29.21): "Therefore, sirs, you should . . . yourselves therefore be none the less eager for toil and the distinction it brings . . . Come then, train zealously and toil hard, the younger men in the belief that this man's place has been left to them, the older in a way that befits their own achievements; yes, and take all the pride in these things that men should who live for praise and glory (πρὸς ἔπαινον καὶ δόξαν ἀγαθὴν βιοῦντας) and are devotees of virtue." 4 Maccabees, which refers to itself as a "demonstration" (ἐπίδειξις, 1:10), also closes with an exhortation, urging the same fidelity to Torah exhibited by the martyrs which are praised throughout that speech: "O Israelites, offspring of the seed of Abraham, obey this law and exercise piety in every way, knowing that pious reason is master of the passions, not only of suffering from within, but also of those from without" (18:1; NRSV).

16 From the *Rhetorica ad Herennium* 3.2.3, one finds that the deliberative orator actually has two goals in mind, namely establishing that a course of action will bring both security and honor. From the author's continuing discussion, however, it is clear that one would never admit that the course one recommended was dishonorable, although one might admit that it was the less safe. Aristotle will multiply the number of "motives of choice" to three: the noble, the beneficial, and the pleasant (*Nicomachian Ethics* 2.3.7). He does not comment as to which would be the leading principle for all hearers, although he prefers the first, as does Quintilian (*Institutio Oratoria* 3.8.1). While a number of factors might thus enter into deliberations, the question of honor figures prominently in all deliberations.

17 This is most fully developed in *Rhet. Her.* 3.2.3–3.4.7. The specific suggestions for what could be included under each virtue bears some striking similarities with the content of Hebrews.

18   This, and the contrary (namely holding up figures of the past for censure as a means of dissuading the audience from repeating their mistakes), figure prominently in Heb 3:7–4:11 and 10:32–12:3, as we shall discuss in chapters three and four below.

19   *Rh.* 1.2.5: "The orator persuades by means of his hearers, when they are roused to emotion by his speech; for the judgements we deliver are not the same when we are influenced by joy or sorrow, love or hate." Cf. also *Rh.* 2.1.8–9 "The emotions (πάθη) are all those affections which cause men to change their opinion in regard to their judgements." Quintilian (*Inst. Orat.* 8.12) continues to stress the importance of this mode of proof: "As regards appeals to the emotions, these are especially necessary in deliberative oratory. Anger has frequently to be excited or assuaged and the minds of the audience have to be swayed to fear, ambition, hatred, reconciliation."

20   Jewish authors of the second and first centuries BCE (e.g., the authors of Wisdom of Solomon and 4 Maccabees) employ the same procedures when seeking to motivate their readers to maintain their Jewish identity and fidelity to the Torah, rather than succumb to the pressures to Hellenize (that is, abandon Jewish exclusivism and take up the Greek way of life, including participation in the pagan cultic activities which were part of the everyday social, political, and civic activities of the Greco-Roman world. For a fuller discussion of the use of honor and shame language in Jewish minority cultural writings, the interested reader may refer to D. A. deSilva, "The Wisdom of Ben Sira: Honor, Shame, and the Maintenance of Minority Cultural Values" (*Catholic Biblical Quarterly* 58 [1996] 433–455) and "The Noble Contest: Honor, Shame, and the Rhetorical Strategy of 4 Maccabees" (*Journal for the Study of the Pseudepigrapha* 13 [1995] 31–57).

21   Cf. 4 Macc 5:22–24, in which Eleazar similarly names the Jewish Torah as the means to education and exercise in the cardinal virtues of justice, piety, temperance, and courage—virtues recognized and esteemed by Eleazar's Greek antagonists—and hence the truer path to honor.

Chapter 2

1   See, for example, G. Hughes, *Hebrews and Hermeneutics* (Cambridge: University Press, 1979), 28.

2   Cf. William Lane, *Hebrews: A Call to Commitment* (Peabody, MA: Hendrickson, 1985), 22–25, and the introduction to W. Lane, *Hebrews 1–8* (Dallas: Word, 1991).

3   T. Schmidt, "Moral Lethargy and the Epistle to the Hebrews," *WTJ* 54 (1992), 167. A similar emphasis appears in W. G. McCown, Ο ΛΟΓΟΣ ΤΗΣ ΠΑΡΑΚΛΗΣΕΩΣ: *The Nature and Function of the Hortatory Sections in the Epistle to the Hebrews* (Ph.D. Dissertation, Union Theological Seminary, VA), 261.

4   H. Attridge, *The Epistle to the Hebrews* (Philadelphia: Fortress, 1989), 13.

5   The pervasiveness of cultic activity throughout all aspects of life in Greco-Roman society has been demonstrated in such works as Ramsay MacMullen, *Paganism in the Roman Empire* (New Haven: Yale, 1981), 38–39, 47.

6   Danker, *Benefactor*, 328.

7   Robert Wilken (*The Christians as the Romans Saw Them* [New Haven, CT: Yale, 1984], 58) underscored the role of piety as the cement of social and political unions: "Piety toward the gods was thought to insure the well-being of the city, to promote a spirit of kinship and mutual responsibility, indeed, to bind together the citizenry. 'In all probability,' wrote Cicero, 'disappearance of piety towards the gods will entail the disappearance of loyalty and social union among men as well, and of justice itself, the queen of all virtues' (*Nat. D.* 1.4)."

8   Suetonius uses this term to describe the Christian group (*Nero* 16), as does Pliny (*Ep.* X.96). The term *superstitio* was also applied to Judaism (Tacitus, *Histories* 5.3–5; Plutarch, *De Superstitione* 8 [*Mor.* 169 C]).

9   Cf. Isocrates, *To Demonicus* 13: "First of all, then, show devotion to the gods, not merely by doing sacrifice, but also by keeping your vows . . . Do honour to the divine power at all times, but especially on occasions of public worship; for thus you will have the reputation both of sacrificing to the gods and of abiding by the laws."

10   Origen, *c. Cels.* 8.75 (*ANF* 4:668).

11   Commentators have consistently recognized this aspect of the addressees' experience (cf. Attridge, *Hebrews*, 299; C. Spicq [*L'Épître aux Hébreux* (Paris: Gabalda, 1952)], 2.329).

12   Cf. G. Kittel, "θεάομαι," *TDNT* 3.43: "The θεάτρον is by human standards, not a proud [spectacle], but a sorry and contemptible." Philo recounts a vivid example of the public nature of punishment in his narration of the brutal actions taken against the Jewish inhabitants of Alexandria in *Against Flaccus* 74–75, 84–85, and 95. Flogging and crucifixion of Jews formed a spectacle and show (ἡ θέα, τὰ πρῶτα τῶν θεαμάτων). Similarly, the record of Nero's execution of Christians in Tacitus's *Annals* 15.44 show that derision was as crucial an element as pain in dealing with that marginal group. The recipients of Hebrews, of course, had not yet experienced such excesses (12:4).

13   Cf. 1 Pet 4:14–16 and Matt 5:11.

14   Chrysostom, commenting on 10:32, notes the power of such disapproval and grants of dishonor to affect judgement: "Reproach is a great thing, and calculated to pervert the soul, and to darken the judgement . . . Since the human race is exceeding vainglorious, therefore it is easily overcome by this" (*NPNF*[1] 14:461; Migne, *PG* 63.149).

15   J. Pitt-Rivers, "Honour and Social Status," 25.

16   Bruce Malina and Jerome Neyrey, "Conflict in Luke-Acts: Labelling and Deviance Theory," in *The Social World of Luke-Acts* (ed. J. H. Neyrey; Peabody: Hendrickson, 1991), 107.

17   This was the mission, for example, of Epaphroditus (Phil 2:25).

18   The imprisoned were aware of the sacrifice made on their behalf, as both "Paul" (2 Tim 1:16) and Ignatius (*Smyrn.* 10) are aware that their visitors had to set aside the disgrace attached to the prisoners' bonds, and risked further injuring their own reputation by associating with the prisoners. Such association could even lead to the sympathizers falling prey to the same treatment, as it did for many Jews in the Alexandrian riots recounted by Philo (*In Flacc.* 72).

19   Cf. Lucian, *Peregr.* 14; Josephus, *The Jewish War* 4.168; Philo *In Flacc.* 5, 53–57.

20   Melito of Sardis, in his "Petition to the Emperor Marcus Aurelius" (cited in Eusebius, *Ecclesiastical History* [tr. G. A. Williamson; London: Penguin, 1965] 4.26.5), bears witness to a sort of open policy for the pillaging of those denounced as Christians:

"Religious people as a body are being harried and persecuted by new edicts all over Asia. Shameless informers out to fill their own pockets are taking advantage of the decrees to pillage openly, plundering inoffensive citizens night and day."

21   Cf. 2 Esdras 16:70–73, which includes such dispossession as part of the persecution of the righteous: "There shall be a great insurrection against those who fear the Lord . . . plundering and destroying those who continue to fear the Lord. For they shall destroy and plunder their goods, and drive them out of their houses."

22   J. Neyrey, *Honor and Shame in the Gospel of Matthew* (Louisville, KY: Westminster John Knox, 1998), 168–173.

23   Neyrey, *Honor and Shame*, 173.

24   Aristotle (*Rh.* 2.6.27) indicates that people "are more likely to be ashamed when they have to be seen and to associate openly with those who are aware of their disgrace." That inhabitants of the Mediterranean world (as any society) were not above taunting their undesirables is shown from such complaints as Ps 108:25: "I am an object of scorn to my accusers; when they see me, they wag their heads."

25   In both 1 John 2:28 and *1 Enoch* 97:1, 6; 98:10, these words are placed within the context of standing before the divine judge at the Parousia or the Last Day. The reward of those who have remained in Christ (or who have continued steadfast in the Law) is "confidence" or "open freedom" before God or Christ, which is contrasted to the shame of the wicked, who are unable to exercise any boldness or openness due to their disgrace before God.

Chapter 3

1   Many translations render this phrase as "perfecter of *our* faith," but this is without support in the Greek. Rather, the author names Jesus as the one who most perfectly embodies the virtue of "faith," and who therefore serves as its best exemplar.

2   So Calvin, *Hebrews*, 91 (commenting on Heb 8:1): "Now, because Christ suffered in the lowliness of the flesh, and, taking the form even of a servant, was made of no reputation in the world, (Phil. 2:7) the Apostle calls us back to his ascension; whereby not only was the ignominy of the cross swallowed up, but also that

mean estate, which he had put on together with our flesh, was thrown off." The taking on of human form was an integral part of Christ's humiliation.

3 So Chrysostom (*NPNF¹* 14:494; Migne, *PG* 63.196): "The blows upon the cheek, the laughter, the insults, the reproaches, the mockeries, all these he indicated by 'contradiction'."

4 M. Hengel, *Crucifixion in the Ancient World* (Philadelphia: Fortress, 1977), 87. Hengel's volume contains a wealth of primary materials documenting the nature, associations of, and reactions to crucifixion in the Greco-Roman and Jewish world.

5 Hengel, *Crucifixion*, 87. Recall also Philo's description of the crucifixion of the Alexandrian Jewish senators as a "spectacle and show."

6 So Delitzsch, *Hebrews*, 306; Lane, *Hebrews 9–13*, 414.

7 Michel, *Hebräerbrief*, 294; Attridge, *Hebrews*, 358 n.72.

8 So R. Bultmann ("Αἰδώς," *TDNT* 1.170): "Shame" is "fear of the αἰσχρόν and therefore of one's δόξα." Strangely, in his article on αἰσχύνη, Bultmann wishes to distance the meaning of this word in the LXX and NT from its meaning in extra-biblical literature.

9 This is, of course, not ignored by modern commentators. Weiß (*Hebräer*, 639) believes this phrase to hold "a parenetic potential" for the addressees, and Attridge (*Hebrews*, 357–58) notes that Christ's "despising shame" serves a "paradigmatic function."

10 Rowan A. Greer (tr.), *Origen* (New York: Paulist, 1979), 68. The Greek clearly shows the literary dependency on Heb 12:2.

11 *NPNF¹* 14:493; Migne, *PG* 63.194.

12 Calvin, *Hebrews*, 169–170. Such a reading is also preferred by Mary Rose D'Angelo (*Moses in the Letter to the Hebrews* [SBLDS 42; Missoula, MN: Scholars Press, 1976] 53), in light of a perceived parallelism with Moses' refusal of a life of ease in Pharaoh's court (11:24–26).

13 This reading is preferred by Delitzsch (*Hebrews*, 306) and Attridge (*Hebrews*, 357).

14 Cf. the praise of the fallen soldiers in Thucydides, *Hist.* 2.35.1–46.2.

15   Cf. Seneca (*Epistles* 24.4) on Socrates' death as liberating humankind from the fear of death.

16   Cf. also Heb 10:19–22.

17   Most notably, David Peterson, *Hebrews and Perfection: An Examination of the Concept of Perfection in the "Epistle to the Hebrews"* (Cambridge: Cambridge University Press, 1982).

18   Cf. H. Moxnes on Paul ("Honour and Righteousness, 68): "It is before God's court that the final decision on honour or shame is made. Thus, the ultimate 'significant other' is God."

19   Recall Pitt-Rivers's observation that, in a complex society, "the individual's worth is not the same in the view of one group as in that of another" ("Honour and Social Status," 22).

20   This ability also distinguishes the "just" from the "ungodly" in Wisdom 1–5.

21   Cf. 2 Cor 4:16–18.

22   Danker, *Benefactor*, 442–443.

23   Danker, *Benefactor*, 443–447. 1 Tim 3:7 demonstrates clearly the sense of "enjoying a good reputation."

24   Cf. Dio, *Or.* 44.1, on being held in honor in one's native land as the highest good.

25   Cf. Dio, *Or.* 66.15; Philo, *In Flacc.* 53–55.

26   The element of choice is important, as D. Worley ("God's Faithfulness," 72–73) has underscored.

27   Cf. Daniel's prayer for the deliverance and vindication of Israel and Jerusalem in Dan 9:18–19.

28   Philo *De vita Mosis* 1.13; Josephus, *Antiquities* 2.9.7.

29   So Lünemann, *Hebrews*, 684; Spicq, *Hébreux*, 357; Josephus, *Antiquities* 2.9.7 §233.

30   Cf. Theophylactus's commentary (Migne, *PG* 125:356): "See, then, how he calls it sin not to endure the like injuries together with one's brothers and sisters."

31   Annotated editions of Hebrews generally refer the reader to 2 Macc 6:18–7:42, where the story of the martyrdoms of Eleazar and the seven brothers is narrated. The strong emphasis through-out 2 Maccabees 7 on the martyrs' expectation of resurrection

demonstrates a clear connection between the texts. The author of Hebrews may also have been familiar with the story as told in 4 Maccabees 5 through 18. Only in this version do the martyrs have the opportunity to be *released* from their tortures in they recant after the slow execution begins (4 Macc 6:12–23; 9:16). Additionally, several phrases in Hebrews echo 4 Maccabees (Cf. 4 Macc 6:9 with Heb 12:2; 4 Macc 17:4 with Heb 3:6, 14.

32   "Better" creates a contrast between the life and enjoyments of this world and those of the world to come, along the lines of similar comparisons within Hebrews, such as 10:34 (earthly property over against "better and lasting possessions") and 11:16 (an earthly homeland over against a "better, heavenly" one).

33   First, it indicates the utter lack of any sort of wealth, which was an important correlate of honor; second, the economic state of these "destitute" ones results from their own choices. To unbelievers, then, they would have been thought to have "brought it on themselves," and so experience not only want but disgrace attached to self-inflicted loss (cf. J. H. Neyrey, "Loss of Wealth, Loss of Family, and Loss of Honor," pp. 139–158 in P. F. Esler (ed.) *Modelling Early Christianity* (London: Routledge, 1995), 144.).

34   Cf. Neyrey, "Poverty," 3 n.12: "There are many examples of honor and status displayed in public by the clothing worn: the Essenes at Qumran symbolized their pursuit of radical purity by wearing the 'white robe' (Josephus *BJ* 2.129; Philo *De vita contemplativa* 66). Conversely, prophets like John the Baptizer identified their roles on the margins of society by wearing garments of skin, not cloth woven in households (Mark 1:6; see Heb 11:37–38; Zech 13:4; Josephus *Vita* 11)."

35   Cf. Malina and Neyrey, "Honor and Shame," 27: "Such physical mobility replicates the social behaviour that rejects ascribed status and implies a willingness to be deviant within the broader context. Yet the willingness to be deviant itself becomes a value worthy of honor within the group."

36   *Diss.* 3.22.63, 65: "A Cynic's friend . . . must be another Cynic, in order to be worthy of being counted his friend. He must share with him his sceptre [or staff] and kingdom, and be a worthy ministrant, if he is going to be deemed worthy of friendship . . . Or do you think that if a man as he comes up greets the Cynic, he is the Cynic's friend, and the Cynic will think him worthy to receive him into his house?"

37   Cf. Epictetus, *Diss.* 1.29.50–54: "But the one who has authority over you declares, 'I pronounce you impious and profane'. What has happened to you? 'Nothing'. But if he had passed judgement upon some hypothetical syllogism and had made a declaration, 'I judge the statement, "If it is day, there is light," to be false', what has happened to the hypothetical syllogism? Who is being judged in this case, who has been condemned? The hypothetical syllogism, or the man who has been deceived in his judgement about it? . . . But shall the truly educated man pay attention to an uninstructed person when he passes judgement on what is holy and unholy, and on what is just and unjust?"

38   Cf. 4 Macc 11:4–6; 12:11, 13.

39   Taitus, The Agricola and the Germania (tr. H. Mattingly; Harmondsworth: Penguin, 1948).

40   Cf. also Dio *Or.* 31.66–68.

41   Cf. Josephus *BJ* 6.38: "For shameful were it (αἰσχρὸν γὰρ) that Romans . . . should be outdone, either in strength or courage, by Jews, and that when final victory is in sight and we are enjoying the co-operation of God." The author of Hebrews likewise points to the availability of help from God, a topic intended to evoke confidence (cf. Aristotle *Rh.* 2.5.21), throughout the letter, notably at 4:15–16 and 10:19–23.

42   The possessions which belong to the earthly realm are of less value than those which are afforded in the heavenly realm precisely because only the latter will "abide," or survive the eschatological removal of the "things that can be shaken" (12:27; cf. the "temporary" nature of worldly enjoyment in 11:25).

43   Cf. Philo, *De virtutibus* 37, where the Midianites exhort their women to seduce the men of Israel in order to preserve their nation: "And do not be afraid of the names of concubinage or adultery, as if they would bring shame (αἰσχύνην) upon you, but set against the names (ὀνόματα) the advantages which would ensue from the facts (ἐκ τοῦ πράγματος), by which you will change your evil reputation (ἀδοξίας), which will endure only for a day, into a glory which will never grow old or die (εἰς ἀγήρω καὶ ἀτελεύτητον εὔκλειαν)."

44   So Michel (*Hebräerbrief*, 347) commenting on the exhortation to leave the camp and go outside to Jesus: "Just so it is certain that there, where hostility with the world breaks out, peace with God is truly to be found." Cf. Plato, *Crit.* 44D.

45   Cf. Peterson, *Hebrews and Perfection*, 170.

46   Cf. Dio's use of the example of Heracles in *Or.* 8.28.

47   Cf. Lünemann, *Hebrews*, 703; Calvin, *Hebrews*, 170, commenting on 12:2.

48   Cf. the similar reversal of values in Acts 5:41, where the apostles, having been scourged as a sign of the authorities' disapproval, "rejoiced that they were counted worthy to suffer dishonor for the sake of the name [of Jesus]."

49   Cf. *Prayer of Azariah* 17; Rom 9:33; 10:11; and 1 Pet 2:6, which all take up the promise of Isa 28:16 (LXX) that "those who trust in him will not be put to shame.

49   Cf. Delitzsch, *Hebrews*, 389–90: "To forsake their company and communion for His sake is to involve ourselves not merely in future but in present shame or reproach; but this reproach is the reproach of Christ, a shame which we share with Him, and in bearing which we are made like Him." Cf. also Héring, *Hebrews*, 123: "We too must . . . behave like pilgrims on the earth, like foreigners who must expect to be held in contempt."

Chapter 4

1   Bernard Williams, *Shame and Necessity* (Berkeley: University of California, 1993), 80. "It is natural, and indeed basic to the operation of these feelings, that *nemesis*, and *aidōs* itself, can appear on both sides of a social relation. People have at once a sense of their own honour and a respect for other people's honour; they can feel indignation or other forms of anger when honour is violated, in their own case or someone else's. These are shared sentiments with similar objects, and they serve to bind people together in a community of feeling."

2   The word usually translated by the nebulous term "glory" is, in reality, very closely connected with the term denoting "honor" in the "secular" Greek of the first-century CE. Cf. Plutarch *Quaest. Rom.* 13 (*Mor.* 266F-267A), in which Plutarch binds δόξα and τιμή together as translation equivalents for the single Latin word *honor*.

3   Lane, *Hebrews 1–8*, 16.

4   Malina and Neyrey, "Honor and Shame," 35.

5   R. P. Saller, *Imperial Patronage under the Early Empire* (Cambridge: Cambridge University, 1982), 8–11.

6   Saller, *Patronage*, 16.

7   J. D. Crossan, *The Historical Jesus: The Life of a Mediterranean Jewish Peasant* (San Francisco: Harper Collins, 1991), 65.

8   F. Danker, *Benefactor: An Epigraphic Study of a Graeco-Roman and New Testament Semantic Field* (St. Louis, MO: Clayton Publishing House, 1982) 436; Saller, *Patronage*, 14: "Nothing was baser than an *ingratus amicus*, and ingratitude was seen as just cause for the breaking off of *amicitia*." See Seneca, *De Ben*. 3.1.1; 7.31.1).

9   Saller, *Patronage*, 10. See Seneca *De Ben*. 2.22.1; 2.24.4.

10   Malina and Rohrbaugh, *Social-Science Commentary on the Synoptic Gospels* (Minneapolis: Fortress, 1992) 74–75.

11   J. Boissevain, *Friends of Friends* (Oxford: Oxford University, 1974) 148.

12   Crossan, *Jesus*, 60.

13   G. E. M. de Ste. Croix ("Suffragium: From Vote to Patronage" [*British Journal of Sociology* 5 (1954)] 33–48) cites numerous examples from these authors.

14   Such considerations in the patron-client exchange have an obvious corollary in the church's Christology and soteriology, wherein God, the Patron, regards Christ's clients (i.e., the Christians) not as their lives merit, but according to the merit of Christ.

15   Saller, *Patronage*, 23.

16   The basic meaning of μεσίτης is "one who establishes a relation which would not otherwise exist" (A. Oepke, "μεσίτης," *TDNT* 4.601).

17   Cited in Barbara Levick, *The Government of the Roman Empire: A Sourcebook* (London: Croom Helm, 1985) 150.

18   Levick, *Sourcebook*, 151.

19   Saller, *Patronage*, 59 (emphasis mine).

20   Cf. Fronto, *Ad M. Caes*. 5.34, 37.

21   de Ste. Croix, "Suffragium," 41.

22   Lane, *Hebrews 9–13* (WBC; Dallas, TX: Word, 1991) 225.

23   Lane, *Hebrews 9–13*, 224.

24   Attridge, *Hebrews*, 55.

25   Cf. the meaning of τελειωθεὶς in Wisd 4:10–13, discussed in chapter 3.

26   Cf. Danker, *Benefactor*, 319. Discussing Luke 18:18–30, Danker writes: "To know God is to recognize him as the Chief Benefactor, who will bestow 'treasure in heaven' on those who share their treasure on earth."

27   Cf. G. H. Guthrie, *The Structure of Hebrews: A Text-Linguistic Analysis* (Leiden: E. J. Brill, 1994) 79–82, 103, 144.

28   Malina and Rohrbaugh, *Commentary*, 75.

29   See D. A. deSilva, "Patronage and Reciprocity: The Context of Grace in the New Testament" *Ashland Theological Journal* 31 (1999).

30   Aristotle (*Rh.* 2.5.16) again provides a definition: "Confidence (θαρρεῖν) is the contrary of fear . . . so that the hope of what is salutary is accompanied by an impression that it is quite near at hand" Cf. also *Rh.* 2.5.17: People may be made to feel confident "if remedies are possible, if there are means of help, either great or numerous, or both."

31   E. Schweizer, *Lordship and Discipleship* (SBT 28; Naperville, IL: Alec R. Allenson, Inc., 1960) 72.

32   D. R. Worley, Jr. (*God's Faithfulness to Promise: The Hortatory Use of Commissive Language in Hebrews* [Ph.D. diss., Yale University, 1981]), 87–92.

33   J. D. M. Derrett, *Jesus's Audience: The Social and Psychological Environment in which He Worked* (New York: Seabury, 1977) 41; Danker, *Benefactor*, 436; Saller, *Patronage*, 10.

34   Recall Dio, *Or.* 31.37: "For what is more sacred than honour or gratitude?"

35   Saller, *Patronage*, 12–13.

36   For example, Dio of Prusa delivers an oration on ἀπιστία (*Or.* 74) in which he recommends distrust of other people as a path to safety in human affairs. The companion oration, περὶ πίστεως, speaks of the burdens of being entrusted with some charge or responsibility. Danker (*Benefactor*, 352–53) catalogues several inscriptions in which πίστις refers to "that which is entrusted," such that "faith is required by the one who awaits fulfillment of the obligation that has been accepted by another."

37   Distrust and challenging God are also linked in Wisd 1:2: "God is found by those who do not put him to the test, and manifests himself to those who do not distrust him (μὴ ἀπιστοῦσιν αὐτῷ)."

38   Pseudo-Isocrates (*Ad Demonicum* 22) advises his young friend thus concerning trust: "Consider that you owe it to yourself no less to mistrust bad men than to put your trust in the good (προσήκειν ἡγοῦ τοῖς πονηροῖς ἀπιστεῖν, ὥσπερ τοῖς χρηστοῖς πιστεύειν)."

39   The verb παροξύνω, often translated as "to urge, prick or spur on," or "to provoke, irritate, excite" (*LSJ*) carries definite connotations of contempt, such that the provocation would spring from the understanding that one has been slighted or insulted. This is most clear in LXX Ps 73:10 and 18; Ps 106:11; LXX Isa 5:24; 65:1–7.

40   Lane, *Hebrews 9–13*, 488.

41   Cf. Derrett, *Jesus's Audience*, 44, in which the author defines faith as "unquestioning expectation of a benefit from Yahweh."

42   Cf. Epictetus's understanding (*Diss.* 4.10.14) that neglect for the gifts and faculties given by God to lead a life "according to nature" is equivalent to dishonoring God.

43   Danker, *Benefactor*, 318.

44   Cf. 1 Thess 1:9: "you turned from idols, to serve a true and living God (θεῷ ζῶντι)."

45   Spicq, *L'Épître aux Hébreux* (2 vols; Paris: Gabalda, 1953) 2:325.

46   Cf. Aristotle, *Rh* 2.5.12: Fear is aroused "also when there is no possibility of help or it is not easy to obtain."

47   Thus Danker (*Benefactor*, 450) writes: "That receipt of benefits from a head of state puts one under obligation and loyalty, is well understood in antiquity."

Chapter 5

1   Cf. Pitt-Rivers, "Honour and Status," 27.

2   Cf. Epictetus, *Diss.* 4.5.22; Plato, *Crit.* 44C; Seneca, *Constant.* 13.2, 5; Isa 51:7–8; Wisd 2:1–24; 5:4–6.

3   Cf. Moxnes, "Honor and Righteousness in Romans," 70.

4   The openness of all parts of a person's life to divine scrutiny is a familiar part of the Jewish tradition, as expressed in Psalm 139 or Sir 23:18–19; cf. also Epictetus, *Diss.* 2.8.13–14.

5   Cf. 2 Cor 5:9–10; Epictetus, *Diss.* 1.30.1.

6   For the use of the divine court among Greco-Roman philosophers and Jewish authors, Plato, *Gorg.* 526D-527A, and 2 Macc 6:26 provide fairly typical examples.

7   Moxnes, "Honor and Righteousness," 68.

8   Cf. Plato, *Republic* 516 B-D.

9   P. L. Berger, *The Sacred Canopy* (New York: Doubleday, 1967), 45; cf. also F. V. Filson, *Yesterday: A Study of Hebrews in the Light of Chapter 13* (London: SCM, 1976), 69.

10   Cf. the use of this "invisible court of reputation" in 4 Macc 13:17, where the seven brothers disregard the disgrace before the human court in the hope that "Abraham, Isaac, and Jacob will welcome us, and all the fathers will praise us."

11   Such a distinction is commonly found in minority cultures. Epictetus *Ench.* 24.1 affords a fine example of such explicit differentiation.

12   So Lane, *Hebrews 1–8*, 55; 2 Thess 2:14.

13   Cf. Aratus, *Phaenomena* 5, cited in Acts 17:28. Epictetus (*Diss* 1.3.1, 4) promotes awareness of one's kinship with the divine as the true and most secure basis for self-respect, which consequently frees one from such heavy reliance on the lay society for recognition of one's worth and confirmation of self-respect. Awareness of this kinship with God, Epictetus argues (*Diss.* 1.13.3), transcends the false distinctions and inequalities created by human society.

14   Derrett, *Jesus's Audience*, 38. This passage appeals to a friendship *topos*, as seen in Aristotle (*Eth. Nic.* 8.12.3). Kinship language emphasizes unity and mutual obligation. That Jesus and the believers have a common origin creates a strong bond, a close association between the two parties, such that a Mediterranean hearer would come to expect the relationship between Jesus and the believers as a relationship of friends, who share their assets, who assist one another.

15   Moxnes, "Honor and Shame, 142.

16   Cf. Josephus *BJ* 4.164, 169.

17   Cf. Dan 9:18–19 (RSV): "O my God, incline thy ear and hear; open thy eyes and behold our desolations, and the city *which is called by thy name* . . . Give heed and act; delay not, *for thy own sake*, O my God, because thy city and thy people are *called by thy name*."

18   That one's honor comes from bearing testimony to God, in effect, appears also in Epictetus, *Diss.* 1.29.44–49: "He bestowed this honour upon you and deemed you worthy to be brought forward in order to bear testimony so important."

19   See N. C. Croy, *Endurance in Suffering: Hebrews 12:1–13 in its Rhetorical, Religious, and Philosophical Context* (SNTSMS 98; Cambridge: Cambridge University, 1998) for a definitive treatment of this passage.

20   Cf. Worley, "God's Faithfulness," 55: "This mutual responsibility extends even to a shared suffering (10:34; 11:25; 13:3) in order that there might be a shared inheritance (11:9, 20, 21; 12:14–17)."

21   Calvin (*Hebrews*, 171), commenting on 12:5, recognizes the connection between the signs of God's adoption and God's benefaction displayed in the believers' experience of suffering, such that he can accuse those who wish to avoid this marginalization as "unthankful" in light of the great benefits which they stand to receive by enduring. A similar strategy appears in Wisd 3:5, where the shameful death suffered on behalf of righteousness becomes the divine discipline by which God tests and proves the worth of an individual and fits him or her to become the recipient of God's eternal benefits.

22   Chrysostom on 10:32, *NPNF*[1] 14:461; Migne, *PG* 63.149.

23   Cf. Spicq, *Hébreux*, 2:385.

24   For a detailed discussion, see the classic study by Victor C. Pfitzner, *Paul and the Agon Motif: Traditional Athletic Imagery in the Pauline Literature* (Leiden: Brill, 1967); Croy, *Endurance*, 37–77.

25   Cf. Thompson, *Beginnings of Christian Philosophy*, 64: "Both Philo and 4 Maccabees belong to a minority culture which was subject to persecution and acts of violence. Because they identified with this minority culture, the image of the contest was a useful way of giving a positive interpretation of the fate of their people."

26   Cf. John Chrysostom (*NPNF¹*, 14:384; Migne, *PG* 63.40.):
"Seest thou that to suffer affliction is not the portion of those who
are utterly forsaken; if indeed it was by this that God first honored
His Son, by leading Him through sufferings?"

27   This is the meaning of the "base unbelieving heart" (καρδία
πονηρὰ ἀπιστίας) of 3:12—the ignoble person fails to recognize the worth and reliability of the divine Patron (cf. Danker,
Benefactor, 318).

28   Chrysostom on 12:16, *NPNF¹* 14:506; Migne, *PG* 63.214.

29   Cf. Moxnes, "Honor and Righteousness," 73: "Power in
weakness, confidence of honour while seemingly put to
shame—that was the paradox of Christian existence in a Jewish
and Greco-Roman environment . . . When Paul urges them to live
a life sharing the sufferings of Jesus (Rom 8:17), he asks them to
live as 'sons without honour'. Therefore, they look forward to the
eschatological moment when they will be glorified with Jesus.
Then the entire world will recognize their honour."

30   Worley, "God's Faithfulness," 92.

31   The possessions which the believers lost in 10:34 are, like the
title and wealth that Moses renounced, of a "temporary"
(πρόσκαιρος, cf. 11:25) nature, in contrast to the "abiding"
(μένων, cf. 10:34; 12:27) quality of their promised inheritance.
Platonic categories emerge in the author's expressions, but these
are completely interwoven with eschatological categories—"that
which abides" is that which survives the eschatological "shaking" of
12:27.

32   Cf. *Rhet. ad Her.* 3.2.3–5.

33   The author thus exhorts the believers to demonstrate Courage (cf. *Rhet. Her.* 3.3.5), transposed form worldly endeavors or
battles to the contest for eternal life.

Annotated Bibliography

Harold W. Attridge. *The Epistle to the Hebrews.*
Philadelphia: Fortress, 1989.

   A fine scholarly commentary on the letter, particularly for those who have access to a library containing the complete Loeb Classical Library and a generous collection of ancient Jewish authors, in order to make use of the many references Attridge provides to background literature for the elucidation of Hebrews' vocabulary and conceptual world.

Frederick W. Danker. *Benefactor: Epigraphic Study of a Graeco-Roman and New Testament Semantic Field.* St.
Louis, MO: Clayton Publishing House, 1982.

   Danker has compiled more than fifty inscriptions from the Greco-Roman period and applied a careful analysis of their terminology to the New Testament documents. From his work, the reader will arrive at a detailed picture of the realm of language related to patron-client relations and its pervasiveness throughout the New Testament.

George A. Kennedy. *New Testament Interpretation through Rhetorical Criticism.* Chapel Hill, NC: University of North Carolina, 1984.

   For those interested in pursuing a deeper appreciation for rhetorical criticism and its fruitfulness for investigating New Testament texts, this is the place to start. Kennedy introduces the readers to the basics of classical rhetorical theory, and takes them through each of the three major genres (deliberative, epideictic, and judicial) with reference to the analysis of actual books of the New Testament.

William Lane. *Hebrews 1–8* and *Hebrews 9–13*. Word
Biblical Commentaries. Dallas, TX: Word, 1991.

Perhaps the most complete commentary on Hebrews
currently on the market, Lane provides a thorough introduction to the letter as well as a theologically sensitive
commentary on the text. He is especially helpful in discussing well-selected parallels from the Greco-Roman and
Jewish literature of the centuries around the turn of the
era as part of his explication of key terms and concepts in
Hebrews.

Halvor Moxnes. "Honor and Shame." *Biblical Theology
Bulletin* 23 (1993) 167–176.

Moxnes has put together a sort of primer on
honor/shame analysis and New Testament texts, compete
with a helpful bibliography for further study. The journal
in which it appears has begun to show a marked interest in
cultural-anthropological interpretation of Scripture.

Jerome H. Neyrey (ed.). *The Social World of Luke-Acts*.
Peabody, MA: Hendrickson, 1991.

This collection of thirteen essays lays out twelve models developed from cultural anthropological studies and
demonstrates their usefulness for biblical interpretation
through providing readings of Luke-Acts from the perspective of each model. Among the models, one will find
helpful treatments of honor and shame, patron-client
relations, labeling and deviance theory, and purity codes.

Julian Pitt-Rivers. "Honour and Social Status," in J. G.
Peristiany (ed.), *Honour and Shame: The Values of
Mediterranean Society*. London: Weidenfeld and Nicolson,
1965.

This is the seminal study which led to the blossoming
of interest in honor and shame as pivotal values in the
ancient Mediterranean among biblical scholars.

Richard Saller. *Personal Patronage under the Early Empire.*
Cambridge: Cambridge University, 1982.
    Saller provides a valuable starting point for the study
of patron-client relations in the Roman Imperial world.
Bringing together a wealth of data from letters and
inscriptions, he traces out the contours of this pervasive
system.

Robert L. Wilken. *The Christians as the Romans Saw Them.*
New Haven, CT: Yale, 1984.
    Wilken offers a careful and thorough look at how
Christians were viewed by their Greco-Roman neighbors.
He approaches this task both through careful analysis of
several major sources on Christians (e.g., Pliny, Celsus,
and Galen) as well as through several constructive essays
utilizing a wide array of comments made by pagans about
these "deviants." The result is a very balanced array of
both positive and negative estimations of Christians by
their neighbors.

Selected Bibliography

Adkins, A. W. *Merit and Responsibility: A Study in Greek Values.* Oxford: Oxford University, 1960.

Anderson, C. P. "The Setting of the Epistle to the Hebrews." Ph.D. diss., Columbia University, 1969.

Anderson, H. "4 Maccabees (First Century A.D.). A New Translation and Introduction," pp. 531–564 in *The Old Testament Pseudepigrapha* (ed. J. H. Charlesworth). Vol. 2. Garden City, NY: Doubleday, 1985. "Maccabees, Books of: Fourth Maccabees," pp. 452–43 in *The Anchor Bible Dictionary* (ed. D. N. Freedman). Vol. 4. New York: Doubleday, 1992.

Attridge, H. W. *The Epistle to the Hebrews.* Philadelphia: Fortress, 1989.

_____. "Paraenesis in a Homily (λόγος παρακλήσεως): The Possible Location of, and Socialization in, the 'Epistle to the Hebrews'." *Semeia* 50 (1990) 211–26.

Barrett, C. K. "The Eschatology in the Epistle to the Hebrews," in *The Background of the New Testament and Its Eschatology* (ed. W. D. Davies and D. Daube). Cambridge: Cambridge University, 1954.

Berger, P. L. *The Sacred Canopy.* New York: Doubleday, 1967.

_____. and T. Luckmann. *The Social Construction of Reality.* New York: Anchor, 1967.

Boissevain, Jeremy. *Friends of Friends: Networks, Manipulators and Coalitions.* New York: St. Martin's, 1974.

Bruce, F. F. *The Epistle to the Hebrews.* NICNT. Grand Rapids: Eerdmans, 1990 [1964].

Buchanan, G. W. *To The Hebrews.* New York: Doubleday, 1972.

Bultmann, Rudolf. "Αἰδώς." *TDNT* 1:169–171. Grand Rapids: Eerdmans, 1964.

_____. "Αἰσχύνω, etc." *TDNT* 1:189–191. Grand Rapids: Eerdmans, 1964.

Calvin, John. *Calvin's Commentary on the Epistle to the Hebrews.* Tr. "by a beneficed Clergyman of the Church of England." London: Cornish and Co, 1842.

Collins, J. J. *Between Athens and Jerusalem.* New York: Crossroad, 1983.

Cosby, M. R. *The Rhetorical Composition and Function of Hebrews 11 in Light of Example Lists in Antiquity.* Macon: Mercer University, 1988.

Crossan, John D. *The Historical Jesus: The Life of a Mediterranean Jewish Peasant.* San Francisco: Harper Collins, 1991.

Croy, N. C. *Endurance in Suffering: Hebrews 12:1–13 in its Rhetorical, Religious, and Philosophical Context.* SNTSMS 98. Cambridge: Cambridge University, 1998.

Danker, Frederick W. *Benefactor: Epigraphic Study of a Graeco-Roman and New Testament Semantic Field.* St. Louis, MO: Clayton Publishing House, 1982.

Davis, John. *The People of the Mediterranean: An Essay in Comparative Social Anthropology.* London: Routledge & Kegan Paul, 1977.

de Ste. Croix, G. E. M. "Suffragium: From Vote to Patronage." *British Journal of Sociology* 5 (1954) 33–48.

Delitzsch, Franz. *Commentary on the Epistle to the Hebrews.* 2 vols. Tr. T. L. Kingsbury. Edinburgh: Clark, 1871–72 [1857].

Derrett, J. D. M. *Jesus's Audience: The Social and Psychological Environment in which He Worked.* New York: Seabury, 1973.

deSilva, D. A. *The Hope of Glory: Honor Discourse and New Testament Interpretation.* Collegeville: Liturgical Press, 1999.

Dodds, E. R. *The Greeks and the Irrational.* Berkeley: University of California, 1966.

Droge, A. J. and J. D. Tabor. *A Noble Death: Suicide and Martyrdom among Christians and Jews in Antiquity.* San Francisco: Harper, 1992.

Ellingworth, P. *The Epistle to the Hebrews.* Grand Rapids: Eerdmans, 1993.

Elliott, J. H. *A Home for the Homeless: A Social-Scientific Investigation of 1 Peter*. Minneapolis: Fortress, 1990 [1981].

Filson, F. V. *'Yesterday': A Study of Hebrews in the Light of Chapter 13*. London: SCM, 1967.

Gilmore, D. D. "Introduction: The Shame of Dishonor," pp. 2–21 in D. D. Gilmore (ed.), *Honor and Shame and the Unity of the Mediterranean*. Washington: American Anthropological Association, 1987.

Guthrie, G. H. *The Structure of Hebrews: A Text-linguistic Analysis*. Leiden: Brill, 1994.

Hadas, Moses. *The Third and Fourth Books of Maccabees*. New York: Harper, 1953.

Hay, D. M. *Glory at the Right Hand: Psalm 110 in Early Christianity*. SBLMS 18. Nashville: Abingdon, 1973.

Hengel, Martin. *Crucifixion in the Ancient World and the Folly of the Message of the Cross*. Philadelphia: Fortress, 1977.

Héring, Jean. *The Epistle to the Hebrews*. Tr. A. W. Heathcote. London: Epworth, 1970.

Hughes, Graham. *Hebrews and Hermeneutics*. SNTSMS, 36. Cambridge: Cambridge University, 1979.

Hughes, P. E. *A Commentary on the Epistle to the Hebrews*. Grand Rapids: Eerdmans, 1977.

Hurst, L. D. *The Epistle to the Hebrews: Its Background of Thought*. SNTSMS 65. Cambridge: Cambridge University, 1990.

_____. "The Christology of Hebrews 1 and 2," in L. D. Hurst and N. T. Wright, *The Glory of Christ in the New Testament: Studies in Christology*. Oxford: Clarendon, 1987.

Käsemann, Ernst. *The Wandering People of God: An Investigation of the Letter to the Hebrews*. Minneapolis: Augsburg, 1984 [1961].

Kee, H. C. "The Linguistic Background of 'Shame' in the New Testament," pp. 133–148 in M. Black and W. A. Smalley (eds.), *On Language, Culture, and Religion: In Honor of Eugene A. Nida*. The Hague: Mouton, 1974.

Kennedy, G. A. *New Testament Interpretation through Rhetorical Criticism*. Chapel Hill, NC: University of North Carolina, 1984.

Kittel, Gerhard. "Δοκέω, δόξα." *TDNT* 2:232–255. Grand Rapids: Eerdmans, 1964.

Kümmel, W. G. *Introduction to the New Testament*. Nashville: Abingdon, 1973.

Lane, W. L. *Hebrews: A Call to Commitment*. Peabody: Hendrickson, 1985.

_____. *Hebrews 1–8*. WBC 47A. Dallas: Word Books, 1991.

_____. *Hebrews 9–13*. WBC 47B. Dallas: Word Books, 1991.

Levick, Barbara. *The Government of the Roman Empire: A Sourcebook*. London: Croom Helm, 1985.

Lindars, Barnabas. *The Theology of the Letter to the Hebrews*. Cambridge: Cambridge University, 1991.

_____. "The Rhetorical Structure of Hebrews." *NTS* 35 (1989) 382–406.

Lünemann, Gerhard. *Kritisch-exegetischer Handbuch über den Hebräerbrief*. MeyerK 13. Göttingen: Vandenhoeck & Ruprecht, 1878.

Mack, Burton. *Rhetoric and the New Testament*. Minneapolis: Augsburg Fortress, 1990.

MacMullen, Ramsey. *Paganism in the Roman Empire*. New Haven: Yale, 1981.

Malina, Bruce. *The New Testament World: Insights from Cultural Anthropology*. Louisville: Westminster/John Knox, 1993 [1981].

_____ and J. H. Neyrey. "Honor and Shame in Luke-Acts: Pivotal Values of the Mediterranean World," in J. H. Neyrey (ed.), *The Social World of Luke-Acts: Models for Interpretation*. Peabody: Hendrickson, 1991.

_____ and J. H. Neyrey. "First-Century Personality: Dyadic, Not Individualistic," in J. H. Neyrey (ed.), *The Social World of Luke-Acts: Models for Interpretation*. Peabody: Hendrickson, 1991.

_____ and J. H. Neyrey. "Conflict in Luke-Acts: Labelling and Deviance Theory," in J. H. Neyrey (ed.), *The Social World of Luke-Acts: Models for Interpretation*. Peabody: Hendrickson, 1991.

_____ and R. Rohrbaugh. *Social-Science Commentary on the Synoptic Gospels*. Minneapolis: Fortress, 1992.

Michel, Otto. *Der Brief an die Hebräer*. 12th ed. MeyerK 13. Göttingen: Vandenhoeck & Ruprecht, 1960.

Moffatt, J. *Hebrews*. ICC. Edinburgh: T. & T. Clark, 1924.

Moxnes, Halvor. "Honor and Shame." *BTB* 23 (1993) 167–176.

_____. "Honor, Shame, and the Outside World in Paul's Letter to the Romans," in J. Neusner, P. Borgen, E. S. Frerichs, and R. Horsley (eds.), *The Social World of Formative Christianity and Judaism*. Philadelphia: Fortress, 1988.

_____. "Honour and Righteousness in Romans." *JSNT* 32 (1988) 61–77.

Neyrey, J. H. "Despising the Shame of the Cross: Honor and Shame in the Johannine Passion Narrative." *Semeia*, 68 (1996) 113–137..

_____. "Poverty and Loss of Honor in Matthew's Beatitudes: Poverty as Cultural, Not Merely Economic Phenomenon." An unpublished paper delivered at the CJA Seminar in October 1992.

_____. *2 Peter, Jude*. New York: Doubleday, 1993.

Nickelsburg, G. W. E. *Jewish Literature Between the Bible and the Mishnah*. Philadelphia: Fortress, 1981.

Olbricht, T. "Hebrews as Amplification," pp. 375–387 in *Rhetoric and the New Testament* (ed. S. E. Porter and T. H. Olbricht). JSNTSS 90. Sheffield: Sheffield Academic Press, 1993.

Peristiany, J. G. (ed.). *Honour and Shame: The Values of Mediterranean Society*. Chicago: University of Chicago, 1966.

Peterson, David. *Hebrews and Perfection: An Examination of the Concept of Perfection in the 'Epistle to the Hebrews'*. SNTSMS 47. Cambridge: Cambridge University, 1982.

Pfitzner, V. C. *Paul and the Agon Motif: Traditional Athletic Imagery in the Pauline Literature*. Leiden: E. J. Brill, 1967.

Pitt-Rivers, Julian. "Honour and Social Status," in J. G. Peristiany (ed.), *Honour and Shame· The Values of Mediterranean Society*. London: Weidenfeld and Nicolson, 1965.

Robbins, V. K. "Rhetoric and Culture: Exploring Types of
    Cultural Rhetoric in a Text," in *Rhetoric and the New
    Testament* (ed. S. E. Porter and T. H. Olbricht). JSNTSS
    90. Sheffield: JSOT, 1993.

_____. "Socio-rhetorical Criticism: Mary, Elizabeth, and the
    Magnificat as a Test Case," pp. 164–209 in *The New
    Literary Criticism and the New Testament* (ed. E. S. Malbon
    and E. McKnight). Sheffield: Sheffield Academic Press,
    1994.

Roberts, K. A. *Religion in Sociological Perspective*. Chicago: Dorsey
    Press, 1984.

_____. "Towards a Generic Concept of Counterculture."
    Sociological Focus 11 (1978) 111–26.

Saller, R. P. *Imperial Patronage under the Early Empire*. Cambridge:
    Cambridge University, 1982.

Schmidt, T. E. "Moral Lethargy and the Epistle to the Hebrews."
    WTJ 54 (1992) 167–173.

Seely, David. *The Noble Death. Graeco-Roman Martyrology and
    Paul's Concept of Salvation*. JSNTSS 28. Sheffield: Sheffield
    Academic Press, 1990.

Silva, Moisés. "Perfection and Eschatology in Hebrews." *WTJ* 39
    (1976) 60–71.

Skehan, P. W., and A. A. Di Lella. *The Wisdom of Ben Sira*. New
    York: Doubleday, 1987.

Spicq, Ceslaus. *L'Épître aux Hébreux*. 2 vols. EBib. Paris: Gabalda,
    1953.

Thompson, J. W. *The Beginnings of Christian Philosophy: The Epistle
    to the Hebrews*. CBQMS, 13. Washington, DC: Catholic
    Biblical Association of America, 1982.

Übelacker, W. G. *Der Hebräerbrief als Appel*. Stockholm: Almqvist
    & Wiksell, 1989.

Vanhoye, A. *Le message de lÉpître aux Hébreux*. Paris: Cerf, 1977.

Weiß, H.-F. *Der Brief an die Hebräer*. 15th ed. MeyerK 13.
    Göttingen: Vandenhoeck & Ruprecht, 1991.

Westcott, B. F. *The Epistle to the Hebrews*. London: Macmillan and
    Co, 1920 [1889].

Wettstein, J. J. Η ΚΑΙΝΗ ΔΙΑΘΗΚΗ: *Novum Testamentum Graecum*, etc. Vol. 2. Amsterdam: Dommer, 1752.

Wilken, R. L. *The Christians as the Romans Saw Them*. New Haven, CT: Yale, 1984.

Williams, Bernard. *Shame and Necessity*. Berkeley: University of California, 1993.

Williamson, Ronald. *Philo and the Epistle to the Hebrews*. Leiden: E. J. Brill, 1970.

_____. "Platonism and Hebrews." *SJT* 16 (1963) 415–24.

Worley, Jr., D. R. "God's Faithfulness to Promise: The Hortatory Use of Commissive Language in Hebrews." Ph.D. diss., Yale University, 1981.

Index of Subjects

A

Aaron; 67
Abel; 79, 102
Abraham; 35, 38, 46, 48–51,
    54–55, 60, 62, 68, 71, 85,
    103, 109, 120, 133
addressees; 5
    as exemplars; 58
adoption into God's family;
    103–104, 113, 134
Aeschylus; 2
Alexandria; 15
    riots; 123
anaphora; 6
angels; 23, 39, 65—66, 68,
    72–74, 78—79, 86–87, 102
anger; 11–12, 69, 121
    of God; 84, 91, 115
anthropology, cultural; 1–2,
    6, 29
Antiochus IV; 55–56, 108
apocalypticism; 1
apocrypha; 38
apostasy; 92, 109
argumentation, forms of; 6–7
Aristotle; 6, 10–12, 42–44, 65,
    77, 80, 848
assimilation; 15, 17
Athens; 2, 8
Aulus Gellius; 90, *see also*
    index of ancient texts

B

Ben Sira; 17
brokers; 70
    relatives as; 73

C

Canaan; 82
Cato the Younger; 41
Celsus; 26–27
Christ; 33, 35, 39, 44, 53–54,
    63, 66, 109, et passim
    as benefactor; 64
    as broker; 75, 116
    as high priest; 68
    as partner; 106, 111
    as benefactor; 34
    as kin; 103
    dignity of; 111
    exaltation of; 109
    reproach of; 53
Christology; 63, 67, 130
Cicero; 70, *see also* index of
    ancient texts
city of God; 50, 60, 76, 79,
    102, 111–112
clothing; 127
    of exemplars; 57
collection for the church; 77
contest imagery; 28–29, 43,
    59, 61, 101, 106–110, 112,
    134–135
countercultures; 15
court; 66
    of Gentiles; 56
    of God; 18–19, 35, 44–45,
      53, 56, 58, 64–65, 68,
      78, 81, 96, 98, 102–103,
      109, 126, 133
    of opinion; 46, 51, 95,
      101, 118
    of reputation; 3, 15, 18,
      35, 38, 42, 52, 95–96,
      98, 99, 101–102, 133

Index of Modern Authors

Index of Ancient Texts

Index of Greek Words

About the Author

David A. deSilva earned a bachelors degree in English from Princeton University, an M.Div. from Princeton Theological Seminary, and a Ph.D. in New Testament from Emory University. He has taught at the Candler School of Theology and is currently associate professor at Ashland Theological Seminary. He has also served as a supply preacher for Lutheran and United Methodist churches and interned at St. George's Episcopal Church in Helmetta, New Jersey. He has written over seventy articles and reviews and has previously published three other books, *Despising Shame: The Social Function of the Rhetoric of Honor and Dishonor in the Epistle to the Hebrews* (Scholars Press, 1995), *4 Maccabees* (Sheffield Academic Press Guides to the Apocrypha and Pseudepigrapha, 1998), *The Credentials of an Apostle* (BIBAL Press, 1998), and *The Hope of Glory: Honor Discourse and New Testament Interpretation* (Liturgical Press). He has three forthcoming books in process: *Perseverance in Gratitude: A Socio-Rhetorical Commentary on Hebrews* (Eerdmans), *Honor, Patronage, Kinship, and Purity: Unlocking New Testament Culture (InterVarsity Press)*, and *Introduction to the Old Testament Apocrypha* (Baker). In addition to his academic pursuits, he has been very active in music ministries throughout his life and is currently director of choirs and organist at Christ United Methodist Church in Ashland, Ohio.